THE
SERVING
SALESPERSON

SEVEN PILLARS TO TRANSFORM
THE CUSTOMER RELATIONSHIP

DANIEL H. MCQUISTON PH.D

The Serving Salesperson

Copyright © 2026 by Daniel H. McQuiston

All Scripture quotations are taken from the Holy Bible, New International Version®, NIV® Copyright ©1973, 1978, 1984, 2011 by Biblica, Inc.® Used by permission. All rights reserved worldwide.

The views and opinions expressed in this book are those of the author and do not necessarily reflect the official policy or position of Illumify Media Global.

Published by
Illumify Media Global
www.IllumifyMedia.com
"Let's bring your book to life!"

Library of Congress Control Number: 2026907206

Paperback ISBN: 978-1-970582-07-9

Cover design by Debbie Lewis

Printed in the United States of America

"I met Dan at Indiana University as a student in his sales & sales management class. He was renowned by the students as the professor everyone wanted. I recall his class being meaningful, challenging and engaging/participatory. During my almost forty-year career in sales and sales leadership, Dan and I remained in contact and his expertise in the sales profession continues to be current and on point. Dan's perspective of putting the customer first in the Seven Pillars of the Serving Salesperson is refreshing and accurate. Sustaining long-term success in sales comes from the customer trusting their sales professional and the customer's business being positively impacted by the product and/or service... leading to repeat sales and referrals.
David Witucki, Fortune 500 Executive Vice-President of Sales

———

"*The Serving Salesperson* calls for a fundamental reorientation of sales—from transactional, winatallcosts behavior to a practice rooted in service, trust, and shared purpose. I had the privilege of learning from Dr. Dan McQuiston as his student at Butler University, where he challenged us to see sales not as a transaction, but as a calling shaped by integrity and care for others. In this book, he brings those lessons to life—offering a timely and practical guide for a profession that has evolved significantly, and for those who believe their work can, and should, serve something greater."
Jennifer Muszik, MTS, Senior Director, Commercial Learning & Leadership Development

———

"Professor McQuiston changed how I thought about sales before I even had a sales job.

I took his class at Butler University not knowing what to expect and left with a completely different picture of what this profession could look like. Dan had a way of cutting through the noise, not just with frameworks and tactics, but with a simple idea that the best salespeople are the ones who genuinely care about the person across the table. That idea stuck. Years later, leading a sales organization at Salesforce, I still find myself coming back to it.

The Serving Salesperson puts that philosophy into words in a way that's both practical and convicting. The Seven Pillars aren't abstract concepts, they gave me new ways to think about how I sell, lead and treat people. As a Christian leader, I saw how naturally the principles from this book align with the Biblical command to put others first.

Dan impressed upon me as a student that success in sales is really just a reflection of how well you've served others. I've found that to be true in ways that go well beyond quota.

Mike Hinker, Area Vice President of Sales, Marketing Cloud, Salesforce

———

"*The Serving Salesperson* offers a refreshing perspective on sales by combining the heart of servant leadership with the purpose of building meaningful customer relationships. It challenges sales professionals to move beyond transactions and focus on serving, guiding, and creating long-term value for others. Dan McQuiston has done it again!"

Tom DeBolt, CEO, Benelli USA

Praise for *The Serving Salesperson*

"In *The Serving Salesperson*, Daniel McQuiston's use of the power of story will resonate deeply with salespeople who have a genuine heart for serving their customers. His research-based Seven Pillars provide sales professionals with a practical way to first cultivate a relationship with customers and then help those customers elevate their thinking. Reading this book will transform you from being mired in problems to envision new possibilities. The Serving Salesperson captures the essence of what meaningful change in sales requires—a salesperson who serves, collaborates, elevates, and guides the customer through their own transformation."
B. Joseph Pine II, author of The Transformation Economy: Guiding Customers to Achieve Their Aspirations

———————

"What if all sales were based on the actual needs of the customer? Dan McQuiston offers a compelling reimagining of what sales can and should be. In *The Serving Salesperson*, the reader finds a powerful, practical framework for building relationships around trust and meeting the needs of customers. This insightful guide is a meaningful contribution to the growing body of servant leadership literature."
Reginald Lewis, Executive Director, Robert K. Greenleaf Center for Servant Leadership at Seton Hall University

———————

"Before any excellent service is delivered or life-changing product reaches an awaiting customer, somebody must make the sale. Selling *is* serving. And yet, selling often gets a bad rap or stresses out the man or woman who must do it day after day. Dr. Daniel McQuiston has cut to the heart of this well-worn paradox, and through *The Serving Salesman,* has given us a deeply human and practical guidebook on how to sell, serve, and remain soulfully human in the pursuit of the worthy calling of sales."

Dr. John Stahl-Wert, internationally best-selling author of *The Serving Leader, and Founder of World Serving Leaders*

———

"*The Serving Salesperson* is more than a book. It's a compass pointing sales back to its true north: service. Daniel McQuiston has written a masterpiece that restores the nobility of selling. His passion for teaching radiates from every page, reminding us that sales isn't about closing deals; it's about opening relationships. As Aristotle once said, '*We are what we repeatedly do. Excellence, then, is not an act, but a habit.*' The author shows us that serving others is the highest habit of the true sales professional.

For those new to selling, this book is a roadmap to authenticity and impact. For seasoned sales leaders, it's a mirror—reflecting that without a customer, we are nothing.

The Serving Salesperson elevates selling from a transaction to a transformation guided by the noble purpose to serve—a must-read for anyone who believes that greatness in sales begins with giving.

Gerhard Gschwandtner, Founder and CEO, *Selling Power* magazine

———

To the Greatest Servant of all

Father, why are we here? I mean, what's our purpose?
Well, James, that's easy. We're put here for service, son, service!
The Reverend James Argus Carmichael McQuiston to his son
W. James McQuiston, circa 1929

In Recognition

Of W. James and Mary E. McQuiston, winners of the *Battle Creek Enquirer and News*'s George Award. Rather than letting the proverbial "George" do it, they did it, tirelessly serving the Battle Creek community in countless ways for over fifty years and setting an example of servanthood for all of us to follow.

Well done, good and faithful servants!

Contents

Preface

I'VE BEEN INVOLVED in sales in one form or another for most of my life. In elementary school, I won the top sales award in my Cub Scout pack for selling light bulbs—yes, light bulbs—door to door. In junior high and high school, I shoveled snow and mowed lawns, eventually expanding into a lawn care service during college. My first job after graduation was selling insurance, and I funded my return to graduate school by running my own painting company for three years.

When I became a university marketing professor—first at Indiana University and later at Butler University—I remained deeply involved in sales. I marketed my speaking, consulting, and sales-training services while participating in dozens of executive education programs. I was also continually "selling" prospective students on choosing Butler as well as advocating for my current students as they pursued internships and sales positions. At the end of my career at Butler I was part of the fundraising team for a new business building, helping raise more than seven figures.

I began teaching sales during my years as a graduate student, and I taught the sales class virtually every semester throughout my entire career. From the very first day, my primary goal was to prepare students to succeed in sales or whatever path they chose. Alongside my academic research, I continually read business articles, white papers, and industry reports to bring fresh insights into the classroom. I also built relationships with sales professionals, consistently observing them and evaluating what truly makes a salesperson successful.

I often asked business professionals who regularly worked with salespeople a simple question: 'What makes a good salesperson?' Over time, the patterns in their answers always seemed to point to the same underlying truth: The salespeople who focused on *serving* their customers were consistently more successful than those who merely *sold* to them. Many went even further than service alone. They helped their customers shift their perspective from problems to possibilities, guiding them to discover new, more aspirational goals. The more I thought about this, the idea to write a book on the topic of what it takes to be a serving salesperson began to take shape

Sometime after that I began to gather the information I needed to write the book. I interviewed more than thirty salespeople whom I or their peers identified as "serving salespeople." From that work emerged what I titled the Seven Practices of Serving Salespeople. As the vision for my book began to crystallize toward the end of my tenure as a marketing professor at Butler, I realized that to gain a more complete picture of a serving salesperson, I needed to gain the perspective of B2B buyers. I wanted to understand the actions and behaviors that buyers experienced and desired from the salespeople that genuinely served them.

I began by interviewing roughly two dozen former students who worked in procurement, asking them to describe the activities and behaviors of salespeople that created value for them. Together with two outstanding research colleagues at Butler, Bob Mackoy and Lova Randrainasolo, we took that information and designed and administered an email questionnaire sent to B2B buyers and received over three hundred responses.

After carefully analyzing the data, the Seven Pillars of a Serving Salesperson emerged. We chose the number seven because, in many traditions, seven signifies completion, fullness, and even divine order. The Seven Pillars emerged from that rigorous research project, supported by my extensive review of white papers, industry reports, topical articles, and corporate research.

My goal with this book is much the same as when I first began teaching: to help salespeople serve their customers more effectively and to guide them into shifting from a problem-focused mindset to a possibility-focused one—discovering their ideal solution and then collaborating to bring that discovery into fruition and transform their operation. My hope is this book helps you do exactly that.

Introduction

CUSTOMERS TODAY EXPECT more from the salespeople who call on them. They're not looking for more choices, more features, or even better products—they can find all of that online in seconds. What they want is for salespeople to move beyond selling and step into serving.

They want someone who takes the time to understand the issues and grasp their implications. They want someone who can elevate their thinking when they're mired in a problem, not by dismissing the struggle but by helping them rise above the noise, see the broader landscape, and recognize possibilities they couldn't see from the ground level. In short, they're looking for a partner who can help them envision solutions that can transform their operation—and perhaps even themselves.

This is the value a Serving Salesperson brings.

While most salespeople approach their interactions with customers with a transaction-oriented mindset, the Serving Salesperson enters with a relationship-oriented mindset. They've forged an internal compass that points toward their true north: serving the customer first. They understand that they cannot transform a customer; the customer must make the choice and undertake the effort to transform themselves. But the Serving Salesperson also knows that before new possibilities can be explored, the relationship must shift from transactional to deeply relational, grounded in authenticity, integrity, and trust. Without that foundation, nothing lasting can grow. With it, everything begins to open.

The framework behind *The Serving Salesperson* emerged from an intensive research project—months of interviews and long hours studying what separates those who merely transact from those who truly serve. A consistent truth surfaced: the most impactful salespeople are the ones who have transformed their own mindset from selling to serving. They approach customer interactions with genuine curiosity, digging to know more by asking thoughtful, purposeful questions. They listen with the intent to understand and are attuned to the nuances and meaning beneath the words. Through that attentive presence, they help customers chart a path forward that feels both possible and genuinely their own.

The insights gained from this research became the basis for a comprehensive electronic survey of B2B buyers. The survey asked not only what they valued most from the salespeople who served them but also what specific behaviors and actions signaled genuine service in their day-to-day interactions. When the data was analyzed, a clear pattern emerged: the Seven Pillars of a Serving Salesperson:

1. **Set Serving as Your True North**
2. **Blend Passion and Perseverance**
3. **Sharpen Your EQ**
4. **Build Trust Through the Human Touch**
5. **Communicate for Impact**
6. **Facilitate the Journey**
7. **Guide the Transformation**

A pillar supports, steadies, and gives shape to a larger structure. In literature and tradition, the number seven symbolizes completeness and purposeful design—a set of ideas forming a coherent whole rather than isolated insights. The Seven Pillars function in exactly this way. Each Pillar illuminates a different dimension of serving, and together they create a solid foundation for the Serving Salesperson. They anchor a serving mindset, forming a framework that guides a behavior built not on tactics but on the deeper work of guiding customers to move from problems toward possibilities.

Because the Seven Pillars speak to who a salesperson becomes—not just what they do—they are best understood through story. A parable lets us watch the Pillars come alive in real conversations, real tensions, and real moments of choice. It offers a more human way to experience the Serving Salesperson framework from the inside out, revealing how the Pillars take root, grow, and ultimately shape a life.

That's why this book is a parable.

In this book a number of truths unfold in the life of someone who doesn't have it all figured out—someone who's frustrated, confused, and increasingly wondering whether there's more to selling than just hitting a number. This story introduces you to someone who senses that their professional struggle is tangled with deeper questions of identity, purpose, and faith.

That someone is Paul Rhodes.

Paul's story is fictional, but the journey he's on is real. When the story opens, his self-absorbed, arrogant, and abrasive approach to selling has left both his professional and personal life in disarray. After a major deal backfires—a collapse triggered by his own failure to be fully truthful with the customer—he's forced to confront the consequences of the shortcuts he's been taking. With his job now at risk, and the security he's always relied on slipping away, he's given one last chance: interview seven Serving Salespeople, each mentoring him in one of the Seven Pillars.

Along the road on his journey, Paul encounters questions, truths, and moments of conviction that reshape not only his professional life but his personal and spiritual life as well. Real transformation rarely stays in one lane.

The hope is that as you follow Paul's story, you'll reflect on your own life—to notice where you've been stretched thin, where you've longed for clarity, and where you've sensed you were made for more than transactions. And perhaps, for you, the Seven Pillars will become not just a framework, but a way of serving that strengthens your work, deepens your relationships, and maybe even steadies something in your soul.

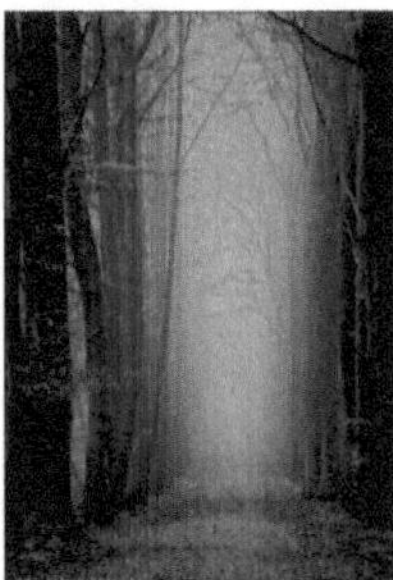

The Road Ahead

The best way to find yourself is to lose yourself in the service of others.

– Mahatma Gandhi

The Meeting

THE FOG THAT had rolled in on the chilly, drizzly, dreary late October morning matched the morning-after fog clouding Paul Rhodes's brain as he held his usual his grande dark roast at his favorite coffee shop. Last night's game had gone into overtime and once again he had over indulged. His buddies bought him beers to help him forget what his wife had told him in their phone call just before he headed out. It didn't work because Mary's voice kept streaming through his head: *Unless you decide to take working on our marriage seriously, I'm going to file for divorce.*

Paul shook his head, partially to come back to reality and partially to get rid of the cobwebs still in there. Walking out to his car, rather than thinking about how his life was going downhill he forced himself back into his ultra-confident—some would say cocky—salesperson persona. He perked up a bit as he thought of his upcoming meeting with

Lew Damon, the president of Petra Industries, the company where he worked.

Meeting with Lew means things are going to get better, Paul thought to himself.

Since joining Petra as a senior account manager four years ago, he and Lew had had a great relationship. Paul really looked up to Lew and even considered him somewhat of a mentor. Early on Lew understood how to deal with Paul's overconfidence and knew how to get through to him. He had taken Paul under his wing and provided advice and encouragement when necessary and reprimanded him when appropriate.

Lew's advice paid off when last week Paul closed one of the largest sales in the company's history with Walters Enterprises. He smiled at himself as he remembered how he overcame all the objections of the buying group, winning them over with his self-described smooth talk. While there were thorny questions, Paul even surprised himself with his ability to finesse his way around all the issues they brought up.

Yep, he thought, *I'm pretty darn good, probably the best we've got. Nobody else here can really hold a candle to me. I pulled off the first step of my plan without a hitch. Now I think three, maybe two, more sales like this one will seal it for me.*

Paul's plan was to position himself to be named Petra's next vice president of sales. Two months ago, Petra's current VP of sales, Gary Wayne, had announced his plan to retire at the end of the fiscal year. That would give Paul several months to close two or three more big sales like the Walters one that he was pretty sure would put him in a position to get the VP job.

Yesterday, Lew called him and asked for a one-on-one meeting. He arrived at the office, parked his car, and made the short walk into corporate headquarters. As he stepped inside the building Paul paused at the mirror by the elevator, straightened his tie, and allowed himself a self-congratulatory smile.

This is what I've worked for. All my effort has finally paid off. Now the entire company is about to know what a good, no great, salesperson I am, he thought as he winked at himself.

He could hardly wait to hear the well-deserved congratulations and accolades from Lew. Why, Lew might even use his accomplishment as an example for the rest of the sales force. The Walters Enterprises order would not only earn Paul a huge commission check, but he also thought this would certainly help to put his name at the top of the list for the VP job.

Yep, I've finally done it. I've earned this! Bring it on!

On the way to Lew's office, Paul walked past Gary Wayne's office, pausing to sneak a peek. *Get used to me,* he thought. *You'll probably be seeing a lot more of me around here before too long.*

Paul confidently walked up to Beth, Lew's administrative assistant, at exactly his appointed time. Beth gave him a quick nod and then picked up the phone and announced to Lew that Paul had arrived. Paul heard Lew's voice say, "Send him right in."

It's show time!

As Paul entered, he was surprised by Lew's demeanor. Paul was expecting Lew to be outgoing and jovial, ready to celebrate Paul's success. Instead, Lew was quiet and reserved, greeting Paul in a pleasant but very subdued manner. Lew directed Paul to sit in a chair across from him at the conference table. Paul was expecting Lew to begin with congratulations or, at the very least, the usual pleasantries, but Lew surprised him by getting right down to business.

"Paul, tell me how you were able to close the sale with Walters."

"I was magnificent," Paul began. "I used all the techniques you taught me. I convinced them we were the best option for their needs. They asked me questions and pressed me on details, and I knocked them all out of the park. Even their curve balls. I was amazing."

Lew listened intently to Paul's story. When Paul had finished, he hesitated for a minute and then looking Paul directly in the eye, said, "Yesterday, I had a conversation with Jim Walters, the president of

Walters Enterprises. Jim and I were roommates in college and have been good friends for over thirty years. It was my relationship with him that got them to consider our product in the first place. Tell me what you told Walters Enterprises about our capacitors, specifically about their performance at temperatures approaching 200 degrees Fahrenheit."

Paul immediately felt the bottom drop out.

The Confrontation

His heart sank and he felt his stomach turn over. All he could do was look down at the floor. His confidence and enthusiasm vanished instantly, and he felt his face becoming flushed. He knew that there was a problem with the capacitors' performance at high temperatures and that he had glossed over it, largely because he felt he probably would have lost the sale if he discussed it in detail. Whenever the engineers at Walters Enterprises brought up the capacitors' tolerance at higher temperatures, he gave them a vague answer, waved it off, and quickly changed the conversation to another topic.

Paul knew there really could be a problem, and that he had done all he could to avoid the issue. He felt like he did in the third grade when he stole a candy bar from the school store and had to go to the principal's office. He had been caught in a lie and he knew it.

When he finally looked up, Lew's steely blue eyes bored right through him. "Well?" he asked.

"I don't know, Lew. I guess ... I guess I didn't think it would be much of an issue, so we really didn't talk about it all that much," Paul stammered, looking back down at the floor.

Even though he was looking down he could still feel Lew's intense gaze. "It certainly is an issue," Lew said firmly, the volume of his voice beginning to rise. "You *know* that our capacitors have been tested to be functionally effective only to 175 degrees Fahrenheit. When operating at 200 degrees for an extended period the insulation begins to break down which renders them inoperable. And if they're not replaced immediately, they can explode. You knew that too, didn't you?" he asked loudly.

Paul frantically searched his mind, trying to find an answer, an excuse, something to say, anything. He opened his mouth to answer but nothing came out. He felt like his entire body was slowly sinking into the carpet. He wished it would.

"The way Walters Enterprises was going to use our capacitors in manufacturing their machines for their customers they could likely have overheated and failed," Lew continued. "And if they did fail it could cause a serious accident in their factories. That would be a financial disaster for both Walters Enterprises and us and would open both of us up to significant liability issues. You knew that too, didn't you?"

"But Lew, those machines almost never reach 200—"

"That's not the point!" Lew shouted, pointing his finger emphatically at Paul. "The point is that they *could* reach 200 degrees, and if they did, all the things I just talked about could happen. And how would you feel about that?"

Paul didn't have an answer. He could only stare at the carpet, too ashamed to meet that steely gaze. After what seemed like an eternity of silence, Lew spoke up. "Besides," he said, his voice surprisingly becoming very quiet in the empathic tone that Paul was used to hearing from Lew. "It's simply not the right thing to do. You really didn't tell them the whole truth about what the product could and couldn't do, did you? Is that *really* the best way to serve your customers?"

Paul's shoulders drooped even more.

"I've also done some checking into some other sales you've made the past year or so," Lew continued. "While you've made your numbers, Paul, there is clearly a pattern of cutting corners. You seem to have fallen into the habit of making the quick buck and moving on, of not taking care of your customers to the best of your ability and not always being truthful. That's simply not the best way to serve our clients and certainly isn't the way we do things here at Petra."

Lew paused for a long moment and then continued. "Paul, you know better than this. And you *are* better than this. You're simply not performing anywhere near what you're capable of, are you?" Before Paul could answer Lew continued, "The order with Walters Enterprises has been canceled."

"They canceled the order?" Paul asked incredulously.

"No! I canceled the order," Lew said. He paused for what seemed like an eternity, waiting for the impact of his statement to sink in. Then with the same quiet and measured tone in his voice he asked, "What do you think is going to happen now, Paul?"

Now What?

Paul's head started spinning. *Now what?* He couldn't believe what was happening. Just a few minutes ago he was on top of the world, scouting out what he thought was going to be his new office, preparing to receive all the praise from Lew for a job well done. Now it looked like he was going to be fired. All sorts of ramifications were racing through his mind—professional, financial, personal—and he sensed the oncoming train wreck. He braced himself for what was coming next.

Lew continued, "Everyone I've discussed this with thinks you should be fired. Everyone, that is, but me. I know what you're capable of. And I also know from talking to Gary that you've been under some personal pressures lately."

You can say that again, thought Paul.

Lew continued. "Quite frankly, the easy thing would be to let you go. This would send a signal to the rest of the sales force and the entire company. However, to get you back on the right track, I have a proposition for you if you're willing to consider it."

Now what? Paul thought again.

Lew sat forward in his chair and continued, "Remember when we had the consulting group come in and conduct the seminar on servant leadership and how the entire management team began implementing those concepts to make us a servant-led company?"

Paul nodded. At first he thought the whole serving leader thing was corny, but after reading the consultant's book and taking some time to let its practices sink in, the company had certainly become an even more pleasant place to work.

Lew sat back in his chair and paused for a bit. Paul could tell he was going to make a point and wanted to choose his words carefully. "For over a year now I've been meeting with a group of successful, servant-led sales managers to determine how we can implement the practices of servant leadership into the selling function of our organizations." Lew's tone changed. He was more upbeat, gesturing with his hands to emphasize his points. "After kicking around several ideas, we hit upon the concept of developing a Serving Salesperson. We researched it carefully and worked with some marketing professors who surveyed business-to-business buyers to find out what behaviors salespeople undertook to serve them better. After we got the results, we had several meetings and discussed at length just what being a Serving Salesperson would entail. These discussions led us to formulating the Seven Pillars of a Serving Salesperson. We chose the number seven because many cultures view the number seven as a symbol of wholeness and completion, and some even associate it with enlightenment and a spiritual awakening."

Lew then handed Paul a laminated cardstock piece of paper the size of a large index card.

The Seven Pillars of a Serving Salesperson

Paul looked down at the card and read:

> ### The Seven Pillars of a Serving Salesperson
>
> 1. **Set Serving as Your True North**
> 2. **Blend Passion and Perseverance**
> 3. **Sharpen Your EQ**
> 4. **Build Trust Through the Human Touch**
> 5. **Communicate for Impact**
> 6. **Facilitate the Journey**
> 7. **Guide the Transformation**

Lew continued to speak, his enthusiasm clearly growing. "We then formed a team to develop an educational program to introduce this concept to our salespeople to assist them into becoming Serving Salespeople. Several members of our group have implemented this program into the sales function of their companies and the results with their salespeople have been very positive. We're going to begin to integrate the practices of these Seven Pillars into our sales force here at Petra, and Paul, I'd like to begin with you. So, what do you say, Paul, are you ready for this?"

Paul quickly ran through the options in his mind. While he wasn't at all sure what it meant to be a Serving Salesperson, it was either accepting Lew's offer or losing his job. He realized he didn't really have much of a choice.

"Thank you, Lew, for giving me a second chance. Of course I'd like to help implement this program here at Petra," Paul said, trying to sound convincing even though he had serious doubts about his ability to become a Serving Salesperson.

Lew stood up, walked over to his desk, picked up a small, spiral-bound booklet, walked back across the room, and handed it to Paul. It had a glossy cardstock cover with the words "The Road to Becoming a Serving Salesperson" printed on it. Inside, Paul found eight tabs, one for each of the Seven Pillars of a Serving Salesperson and one at the end entitled "Putting It All Together". Paul flipped through and noticed the pages were largely blank, but there were a few exercises and diagrams. Lew also referenced a QR code on the back cover.

Oh, man, what have I gotten myself into? thought Paul.

"By scanning the QR code you can go to a website where you can download the contents of the booklet onto your computer," said Lew. "We've designed it so you can take notes either in the booklet or on your computer. We'll talk about how you'll use this booklet in a minute."

Paul looked up with his eyes open wide and suddenly blurted out, "Lew, you've always preached partnering with our customers, and that's what I've tried to do." He clearly was uncomfortable with the direction in which this conversation was headed. "Besides," he continued, "I don't know how comfortable I'd be with being a servant to my customers." In his mind he had already conjured up an image of him dressed in a white waiter's jacket with a linen towel over his arm, bringing out the afternoon tea.

"It's still partnering," Lew said reflectively, relaxing back in his chair, "but we're really taking the entire aspect of partnering to a whole new level. What we're talking about here is embodying a servant's *heart*, not being a personal attendant. There's a big difference."

Where's he going with this? thought Paul.

What we're talking about here is embodying a servant's heart, not being a personal attendant.

Lew continued. "Notice that we're using the term *serving* rather than *servant*. Our group chose the term *serving* because it implies taking an *active* role in the sales process. We also chose this term because a Serving Salesperson is concerned first and foremost with taking a pro-active role in serving the needs of their customers. It means meeting the needs of the customers first and serving them in the best way possible. So far we've found that prioritizing customers with a serving mentality has led to increased sales and profits, particularly in complex sales.

"Your goal as a Serving Salesperson is to go beyond simply diagnosing their needs to truly understanding their needs, their desires, and their objectives. Once you comprehend those needs, you set about serving them by doing whatever you can to help them meet those needs and thereby accomplishing their desired objectives. Most salespeople will stop once they have identified their customers' needs. As a Serving Salesperson, we go past simply meeting the customer's needs. We work to transform our relationship with customers from a transactional exchange to one rooted in the serving posture of the Seven Pillars. When that relationship is genuinely transformed, it creates the opening for us to guide the customer toward transforming their own perspective—the way they think, decide, and act. The Serving Salespeople in other organizations who have practiced the Seven Pillars in their interactions with their customers have had great success in transforming their relationships and moving onto guiding a transformation with their customers."

"Lew sat forward in his chair and continued, "I'm prepared to give you a second chance, but you're going to have to meet some pretty stiff requirements."

What choice do I have? Paul almost said out loud. Instead, he said, "Of course, Lew. I'll do whatever it takes." He tried to sound convincing even though he still had that image of him in a white waiter's jacket in his head.

The Charge

Lew spoke in a more straightforward tone. "If you wish to continue at Petra, Paul, you are going to have to interview all the salespeople on this list." He handed Paul a sheet of paper with seven names, complete with a photo and their contact information. "These folks' contact information is contained in your booklet and at the site the QR code directs you to. Each of these salespeople was part of the group that came up with the Seven Pillars of the Serving Salesperson concept, and they all personify the concept of being a Serving Salesperson. All of them are also working to implement these Pillars of a Serving Salesperson into their own organizations. As I mentioned, so far, the results have far exceeded their expectations.

"You're to meet with each of these seven people at the beginning of the month for the next seven months," Lew continued. "Each one will discuss the behaviors and practices of one of the Seven Pillars of being a Serving Salesperson and how you can implement those practices and behaviors into your sales approach. You're to ask them questions about what they've done to not only understand and meet their clients' needs but to develop the attitude *to* serve not to *be* served. You'll record their thoughts and reflections in this booklet or on your computer. You'll also notice that with each Pillar you'll have some exercises to work through to help you gain a better understanding of their specific Pillar of being a Serving Salesperson. All these folks are dear friends of mine and are members of a group that I meet regularly with called the TBS."

"What's the TBS?" Paul asked with a quizzical look.

Lew's face broke into a mischievous smile. "You'll find out soon enough," he said, with a sudden twinkle in his eye. "All of these folks are expecting a phone call from you to set an appointment, beginning with Matthew Solomon. It's now the end of October. As I said, you're to meet with one TBS member each month for the next seven months. They're all expecting you to contact them to set an appointment to meet with them on one of the first three working days of the month to learn about their respective Pillar of being a Serving Salesperson. They'll give you exercises and suggestions on how to work the principles of that Pillar into your professional and personal life during that month."

Lew continued. "At the end of the month you'll go back to them, show them your work, and discuss with them what you've done to implement the practices of their respective Pillar and how it's impacted your life and made you more of a Serving Salesperson. If the TBS member feels you have grasped the principles of their Pillar sufficiently, he or she will then pass you on to the next member with the phrase *Well done*. You will then go to the next member of the TBS to learn the principles of their Pillar and continue until you have covered all Seven Pillars. When you've completed all seven interviews, you'll come back and see me, and we'll decide where we'll go from there."

Seven Months

Seven months!? thought Paul. *That's an eternity! Seven weeks maybe, but seven months!? This is getting more complicated all the time, and I'm not at all sure about this Serving Salesperson thing.*

Sensing Paul's skepticism, Lew continued, "You're only going to learn about one Pillar a month because this isn't a quick fix. Becoming a Serving Salesperson is not something that's going to happen overnight. It's a process that's going to take time. This is a journey not a destination. This will involve developing a totally different mindset on your part of viewing sales, your customers, and most of all yourself."

Becoming a Serving Salesperson is a journey, not a destination.

There's nothing wrong with my mindset, thought Paul. *Sure, I messed up with Walters, but next time I just need to be more careful and make sure I know the critical information about the customer's application.*

"By interviewing these people and doing these exercises you're going to learn to radically change the way you look at sales and serving your customers," Lew continued. "It's going to take time, patience, and most of all the effort to change not only your attitude but your heart. Changing your heart, Paul, is a continual process. To *act* differently, you need to *think* differently, and this entire process is built around teaching you to think differently."

Seven months! Paul kept repeating it in his mind. *Why do I have to do this for that long? I'm the best salesperson we've got. I always meet my numbers and just made the biggest sale our company's seen in years. There must be some sort of short cut I can take so I'm not spending a lot of time on this.*

Lew continued his explanation. "The salespeople in the other companies who have embraced the Serving Salesperson concept have found that adopting this mindset has not only changed the way they sell but also how they approach their life. They look at the world entirely differently now. I know this sounds like a significant change for you, and it is. But I'm convinced you can do it," said Lew, again in his mentor tone.

Lew paused once again, and Paul could see by the look on his face he was about to say something important.

"There's one other thing I need to mention. You need to know that there will be some spiritual references in the conversations you will have. I just don't want you to feel blindsided when it comes up. Regardless of your views about spiritual matters, understanding the serving aspect is critical. If you're going to be a successful Serving Salesperson, you first must cultivate a *serving* mindset.

"Now, you have an appointment with me on the third Friday in June, a little over seven months from now. Remember, you're to speak with each of these people in the first part of each month and then spend the rest of the month integrating and implementing the practices of their Pillar into your daily activities. As I said, acting differently requires thinking differently. I don't know your feelings on religion, but the Bible says 'Do not be conformed to the pattern of this world, but be transformed by the renewing of your mind."[1] Paul, I have every confidence that interviewing these folks will help you to think differently and help you to be transformed by the renewing of your mind into embracing the philosophy of being a Serving Salesperson. And if your mind is transformed, your heart can be transformed as well."

Really!? Renew my mind!? While Paul managed a weak smile, inside he was dreading the prospect of what was to come. He was already thinking of ways to get around all this work.

Lew stood up, indicating the meeting was over. Paul began to extend his hand, but Lew surprised him by moving over and standing directly in front of Paul. He put his hands on Paul's shoulders. He looked Paul directly in the eye with a serious expression on his face and said softly but firmly, "Paul, I know you can do this. You know that you can do this."

Well, what choice do I have? Paul thought. *Petra is a good company. They pay me well, and besides, if I have to look for another job right now, who's the first person a prospective company would call for a reference? And what'll he say? No, right now I just need to suck it up and figure out how to minimize my effort on these interviews and get out there and get the sales I need to get the VP job.*

Lew took his hands off Paul's shoulders. "I'll look forward to seeing you in about seven months." His voice brought Paul back to the present. "And I'll be anxious to see how this works for you." Lew gave him a firm handshake, and Paul saw that the steely blue eyes had softened. "I know that you're capable, Paul. The best salespeople take the attitude of being a person that comes to serve, and we all want to help you become one of those salespeople."

Lew watched Paul leave and shut his office door. He walked back to his desk, sat down in his chair, settled back, and let out a long sigh.

"I hope I've done the right thing," he said to himself. "I think I have. I just hope I have."

------

1   Romans 12:2.

Realization Hits

Paul's mind was numb as he walked back into the elevator. When the elevator came to a halt on the first floor, Paul found himself standing in the empty lobby unsure of what to do next. He needed time to think, to contemplate what had just happened, to process everything Lew had said, to contemplate his next move. He wandered into a quiet empty area and sat down. While he knew there was an element of truth to what Lew had said, he just didn't think the situation with Walters was as serious as Lew had made it out to be. For a long time, he just stared out the window into the dreary gray morning with a thousand thoughts running through his mind. *Heck, every salesperson stretches the truth sometimes, and a lot of them say things that are a lot worse than I did. Lew made way too much of an issue of the capacitor thing. I've never seen a machine that those capacitors were installed on get anywhere close to two hundred degrees.* Then he remembered that Lew said those who had embraced the Serving Salesperson concept look at the world entirely different now. *Do I need to look at the world differently?* he thought.

Paul's thoughts drifted back to when he first started out in sales. He felt a smile creep over his face. He remembered how he had really looked forward to working with his clients, discovering their needs, helping them meet those needs.

I still do, Paul thought to himself. *Sure, my tactics may have changed, but I'm still pretty successful. I always make my numbers, and I make a good living. While I'm a bit embarrassed with what happened with Walters Enterprises, all salespeople have lost big sales. What I'm more upset about is seeing what would have been a nice commission go down the drain and setting my VP plan back a bit. I'm glad I still have my job, but I wish I had a better idea of what the future looked like.*

Paul leaned back in his chair and let out a long sigh. He sometimes felt that life hadn't been fair to him, and this was one of those times. Sure, he had cut some corners to make other sales, but all salespeople do that.

Also, he had heard whispers around the office that with his ultra-confident persona he was not easy to work with and that people in his department avoided him. If he was going to get that VP job, he was going to have to address that, at least until he got the job.

Then he thought about his relationship with Mary. For the last couple of years, it just seemed that she did not appreciate that all the time he put into his job was for the good of his family. While she was once deeply in love with him and he with her, increasingly she had begun to tell him she did not like the person he had become. She had begun to hold him accountable for his actions, constantly reminding him that while all the material things they were accumulating were nice, she didn't like what his drive to succeed was doing to him, and most of all, to their family. They began to argue, and the arguing had become more frequent and heated. As far as Paul was concerned, Mary just didn't seem to get it.

Finally, one night about eight months ago, during an especially tense argument he had gotten so angry he decided they should separate. He stormed out in a huff the next day and had lived in his own apartment since then. He knew that by living apart he was also growing apart from his two girls, Elizabeth and Ruthie, who were in their busy tween years. While he saw them every other weekend, he had spent those times concentrating on entertaining them, spending money on them, and trying to convince them what a cool dad he was. However, lately they both had begun to comment that rather than being entertained all the time, they would rather have him spend quality time with them, really getting to know them as the young women they were becoming. He was beginning to get the sense that his relationship with both was pretty shallow.

And then there was the ultimatum from Mary last night.

She can't be serious, Paul thought.

And then he began to think about how he was going to deal with trying to be a Serving Salesperson.

I'm pretty good at determining what I need to do to get the job done. When I think about what Lew said, what Mary said, and my relationship with my kids, I really don't see anything major I have to fix. I just need to tweak things a bit. Maybe I do need to be a bit more forthcoming with my customers. I can do that. I can communicate better with Mary, help her a bit more financially, and just try to be a bit nicer to her. I can do that. Spend more time with my girls. I can do that. Nothing major here. I can make some effort, give everyone what they're looking for, and then go back to what I've been doing. I can fake it till I make it.

But there was still the matter of the interviews Lew told him he had to do. He scanned the list of people that Lew had given him. It contained the names of men and women from what appeared to be all types and sizes of companies. *What am I going to learn from them? And what's this TBS group? I'll probably just get a bunch of sales speak from them, so what I'm going to focus on during those interviews is learning just enough to satisfy Lew. Sure, I may learn some things, but is my life really going to change as much as Lew says it will? I really doubt it.*

All these thoughts were jumbled together and running through Paul's mind as he trudged out of the building into the gloomy morning, albeit at a decidedly slower pace than when he walked in.

The doors closed behind him.

Set Serving as Your True North

> *"Take the first step in faith. You don't have to see the whole staircase, just take the first step."*
>
> — *Martin Luther King Jr.*

Beginnings

THE FIRST MONDAY in November found Paul on his way to the office of the first person to interview on his list, Matthew Solomon. Matthew was the president and owner of Integrity Sales, a large manufacturer's representative firm. Paul had met Matthew briefly some time ago on one of his rare visits to church when Mary had dragged him there, but he knew him more by reputation than anything else. Matthew was known as a very successful, hard-working businessperson and was one of those community leaders that everyone looked up to and admired.

Matthew's work ethic had paid handsome dividends as Integrity Sales had grown to around fifty employees with five offices in three states. He had also been president of several civic organizations and was well known not only for his business acumen but also for being an honest and humble individual who ran his company with, well, integrity. He was one of those people that businesspeople wanted to know and seek advice from.

As Paul absentmindedly drove through traffic, he began to feel a bit intimidated at the prospect of meeting with Matthew. He wondered if Matthew knew about the Walters Enterprises situation, and what he would think of him if he did? *Still,* Paul thought to himself, *I just need to learn enough here to satisfy Lew. I'm going to have to walk a fine line here between getting out of there quickly but at the same time giving him the respect he deserves.*

When Paul arrived at Integrity Sales, he walked up to the reception desk. "I'm here to see Mr. Solomon," he said, handing the receptionist his business card. She accepted it with a cheerful smile and replied, "Oh, yes, Mr. Rhodes, Matthew said to send you right up."

Matthew? Not Mr. Solomon?

The cheerful receptionist picked up the phone and punched in a number. "Malisa, would you tell Matthew that I'm sending Mr. Rhodes right up?"

"Here you are, Mr. Rhodes," she said, handing Paul's card back to him. "Take the elevator up to the second floor, turn left when you get off, and go to the end of the hall. Matthew's assistant, Malisa, will meet you there."

"Thank you, Penny," said Paul, seeing her name plate as he turned to head to the elevator. *Wow!* he thought. *She calls me Mr. Rhodes and her boss, who's worth about a jillion times more than I am, she calls Matthew. I wonder how that happens.*

Paul exited the elevator and walked down the hallway to Matthew's office. He looked up to see Malisa waiting to greet him at the end of the hall.

"Matthew will be right with you; I'm afraid he's a bit preoccupied now," she said. "It seems that one of our copy machines is acting up again, and he's down there seeing if he can help fix it." She gestured down the hall to her right to a large working area where Paul saw several people huddled over the copy machine, like so many emergency room doctors working on a patient.

Scanning through the crowd he recognized Matthew in the crowd. He was on his knees on the floor, his sleeves rolled up, reaching up into the machine and slowly, carefully, pulling out a torn sheet of paper. "Try it now," he said. Another person pushed the copy button and as the machine cranked out a copy, Matthew responded with a joyful "Success!" amid hoots and hollers of joy. Getting up off the floor, he looked down the hall and noticed Paul.

"Hi, Paul!" he said with a friendly, cheerful smile and a wave. "Nice to see you again. Give me just a minute to get cleaned up and I'll be right with you. Malisa, please make Paul comfortable until I get there."

As Malisa escorted Paul down the hall to Matthew's office, Paul noticed one wall was almost entirely covered with every sort of award that a manufacturer's representative could win—Rep Firm of the Year, President's Club, 110 Percent Award, and several others. There were also some pictures of Matthew with several VIPs, including some local and even national political and sports figures that Paul recognized. Clearly this was a very successful man, and Paul was even more humbled that Matthew had agreed to spend some time with him. Malisa left Paul in Matthew's office and returned to her desk.

Paul absent-mindedly looked out the window, feeling even more intimidated by meeting with a person of such high esteem and proven business success.

"Did Malisa get you everything you need?"

The First Pillar

Paul was startled as he had not heard Matthew come in.

"Oh yes, she's been very kind, as are you, Mr. Solomon."

"Please, call me Matthew."

"All right, Matthew, I really appreciate the time you're taking to meet with me. I couldn't help but notice the impressive array of awards that you've won."

Matthew appeared to be in his early fifties, tall and stocky with a full head of graying hair. He smiled a gracious smile and said, "It's awards that *we've* won, Paul. Everyone here at Integrity Sales had a hand in earning these awards. We display these so our folks can see the fruits of their labor on a regular basis."

Matthew walked over to a small round conference table. "Have a seat," he said, motioning for Paul to sit in a chair across from him. "You see, Paul, our firm is totally committed to the servant leadership philosophy, and our management team never asks our employees to do anything that we wouldn't do ourselves. We try to serve our employees whenever the opportunity presents itself. It's like me going to fix the copy machine. It just so happens that my first job out of college was selling the very brand of copiers we happen to have, and I still know my way around them well enough to fix the occasional paper jam."

Maybe, just maybe, Paul thought, *there might be something I can learn from Matthew after all. There had to be a reason why Lew chose him to talk about the first Serving Salesperson Pillar of Set Serving as Your True North.*

Leaning forward in his chair and putting his elbows on the table, Matthew began. "Now, Lew tells me that you're learning about the Pillars of being a Serving Salesperson, and I'm to talk to you about the first Pillar: Set Serving as Your True North."

Well, that's not quite how it happened, thought Paul, but instead he answered, choosing his words carefully. "Yes, Matthew, I've had a couple of bumps in the road, and Lew wants me to help our sales force become Serving Salespeople," said Paul, trying to sound convincing.

If Matthew sensed any lack of interest from Paul, he didn't acknowledge it. "Paul, we both know that the field of sales is a roller-coaster ride. You can be high as a kite one day and down in the dumps the next. A lot of it has to do with being bogged down with the everyday firefighting stuff that salespeople face, and that's caused you to lose your focus on serving your customers. Am I right?"

Paul figured it was best to play along, so he nodded in agreement.

Continuing, Matthew said, "What we're here to do, Paul, is to get you back on track. The way to do that is for us to talk about the First Pillar: Set Serving as Your True North. Shall we get started?"

Knowing that he had to show interest, Paul took out his journal and flipped open the first tab which read Set Serving as Your True North.

"Paul, what do you know about the phrase *true north?*"

"Well, I believe it had its origins with some of the early seafaring people who needed a way to guide them on their travels. They needed a reference point, something that didn't change, and they discovered that the North Star would give them the true north that they could always count on to keep them going in the right direction."

"That's right," said Matthew. "And just as sailors needed a true north in a navigational system, so do all individuals need a true north—a set of enduring, unwavering practices that do not change no matter the circumstances. To become a Serving Salesperson, what you need to do is set as your guiding principle—your true north—the practice of putting the customer first and being authentic and genuine as you seek to serve their needs to help them become as successful and profitable as they can be. Setting serving as your guiding force permeates all your interactions with the customer and is a critical first step in transforming your relationship with the customer. It also lays the foundation for all the other Pillars of being a Serving Salesperson. That's why the first Pillar of being a Serving Salesperson is Set Serving as Your True North."

Wow! thought Paul, *I like that analogy. Let's see where this goes.*

Thinking Differently

"Paul, being in sales for as long as I have, I can tell you that most salespeople have a seller's mentality. They enter each sales situation with a mindset to do whatever they need to do to just get the sale. They are there to meet their own or their company's needs, not to meet their customers' needs. And most of them think of selling as a zero-sum game—in order to win someone else has to lose.

"Paul, I'm guessing that Lew told you acting differently requires thinking differently?"

Paul nodded.

"Rather than trying to *sell* to your customers, the mindset of a Serving Salesperson is focused on *serving* them, assisting them to buy. Lew may have mentioned that we need to be transformed by the renewing of your mind. That comes from the Bible, in Romans 12:2. To be a true Serving Salesperson your mind must be transformed, to think differently, and to renew your thought patterns around serving your customer rather than simply trying to sell them something. You need to transform your mind to have a *serving* strategy rather than a *selling* strategy."

A serving strategy? thought Paul.

The Serving Salesperson transforms their mind to have a serving strategy rather than a selling strategy.

Matthew continued, "You're not making *sales* calls; you're making *serving* calls—and serving calls are much more liberating than sales calls. When you make a serving call, your main objective is to focus on *understanding* the needs of your customer, and then work together with them to find the best solution. In a serving call, you're freed from constantly maneuvering the customer toward purchasing your product. If you're focused on serving their needs, oftentimes the next step will usually become evident quickly."

"And being a Serving Salesperson offers that?" Paul asked, surprising himself with how this novel approach was beginning to pique his interest.

"It truly does," replied Matthew. "Let's do this. Tell me about the last time you served, really served, one of your customers, when you were totally focused on meeting their needs. That was the only thing that mattered, and time and cost were secondary issues."

Paul had to think for a while because it had been some time since he had done anything like that. He finally thought of an example the summer before last when he had received an emergency phone call from a customer late on a Friday afternoon. The customer needed a machine fixed to meet a rush order for one of their important customers. Paul had bowed out of his golf game, got the parts needed to fix the machine, and picked up one of Petra's engineers. They went to the customer's plant and fixed the machine so the customer could run the machine over the weekend to fulfill the order.

Matthew smiled approvingly. "Now," he said, "tell me how you felt when you completed that process."

An Internal Compass

"I remember feeling pretty good that I was able to solve the customer's problem," Paul admitted. He smiled as he remembered the plant manager shaking his hand and thanking him for his efforts. "The plant manager even called Lew to tell him what I had done and how his big order had been saved. I guess you could say that I felt as though I'd not only done my job but had gone above and beyond the call of duty. Would that be an example of setting your true north around serving the customer?" He had to make sure that he had the right information to show to Lew.

"Yes, it would be, and it's vitally important to think like that," Matthew answered, again leaning forward with his elbows on the table and a satisfied grin on his face. "Because if we don't set our true north, set our own direction for both our professional and personal lives, someone else—our company, our boss, the people around us, social media, you name it—will set it for us. Then we'll spend all our time following the direction that others have set for us rather than proactively determining the course of our own lives."

Looking up from his journal Paul said, "Are you talking about having sort of a road map?"

"No, we're not talking about a road map but a compass, an internal compass," Matthew said thoughtfully. "A road map only lays out any number of directions you can go. But your own internal compass always points to your own true north—those enduring, unchanging practices that do not change no matter the circumstances. We either set our own course, our own true north, or we spend our lives following someone else's. There's really no in between."

> *Your own internal compass always points to your own true north—those enduring, unchanging practices that do not change no matter the circumstances.*

Paul felt like he'd just been hit over the head with a two-by-four. He realized that he had never really sat down to think about his life's purpose, what direction his life should take, and what actions he needed to take to get there. He also realized his attitude toward this session with Matthew was shifting a bit, and maybe, just maybe, he could come away with some information he could use, something that would help him get the VP job. Matthew had made him feel comfortable enough to ask the question that was on his mind.

"So, how do we set our true north, Matthew? And how do we know we're on the right course?"

"We must look at what guides our lives, Paul, what our personal mission is going to be. We need to decide what direction we want to take in our lives and determine how we're going to get there. The things that you let guide your life—your true north—will dictate every aspect of not only your professional life but your personal life as well. Now, let me ask you a question." Matthew paused to make sure he had Paul's full attention. "Do you have a personal mission?"

Determining Your Mission

The impact of that question hit Paul over the head even harder than the previous one. He winced and suddenly found himself becoming very uncomfortable, shifting around in his chair. He thought of the conversations—no, arguments—where Mary had told him time and again how he was neglecting his family, his relationships, and everything else that once had been a priority in his life to pursue that one more sale, that larger paycheck, the added recognition, that thing he felt he needed. Rather than answering, he hedged and said, "You know, I really hadn't given it much thought."

He looked up to find Matthew looking at him with a penetrating stare, expecting a better answer than that. Not having one, Paul quickly changed the direction of the conversation. "How did you set your true north, Matthew?"

Giving Paul the grace to change the direction of the conversation, Matthew again relaxed in this chair. "Have you ever heard of ABC selling—always be closing?"

Paul nodded. That had been his mantra for several years.

"When I started my business, I decided that was not going to be my mission. Instead, I changed it from ABC selling to ABS—always be serving. I started with that as my personal mission almost thirty years ago, and I still attempt to integrate it into every phase of my life. A long time ago I wrote my personal mission statement—my own personal true north—which spells out the behaviors and practices that I wanted to govern my life."

Paul surprised himself by realizing how much he was being drawn in by the direction of the conversation. "I've never thought about having a personal mission statement," said Paul. "Would you mind giving me some idea of what a personal mission statement should look like?"

"I can do better than that," answered Matthew. He turned around and opened a drawer in his credenza. He reached in and pulled out a piece of paper and handed it to Paul. "Here is my mission statement. Feel free to use it as a model or to inspire your own."

Paul read the statement and noticed phrases that they had been discussing: being a servant to those most precious to him, showing authenticity, walking with integrity, and caring about his customers' business as much as his own. As Paul finished reading, he understood further why Matthew had the reputation he had. Looking up, Paul asked, "How did you happen to choose being a servant as the guiding practice of your life?"

"I discovered that when I focus on serving those around me, it positively affects virtually every element of my life, and I find fulfillment in what I do," Matthew said. "Once you set your true north around having a mission of serving your customers, it gives you a standard by which to judge your progress. You are guided by your internal compass that enables you to see where you want to go and how you want to get there."

Wow! Paul thought, *I've never thought of this. This is something I think I might be able to use.*

The Devoted Giver

"Let's talk more about having a serving mindset," Matthew continued. "I recently read a book about having success in the workplace. It said that success depends largely on the type of reciprocity styles that individuals employ in their interactions with other people. This research identified three types of reciprocity styles:

Takers – those who put their own interests ahead of others' needs.

Matchers – those who strive to preserve an equal balance of giving and taking.

Givers – those who prefer to give more than they take.

"And here's the main point: when reciprocity styles across cultures in countries all over the world were studied, there was one style that is truly universal. The majority of people across a wide range of cultures endorse *giving* as their single most important guiding principle. People in all the countries surveyed reported caring more about giving to others than about power, achievement, excitement, freedom, tradition, conformity, security, and pleasure.

"My colleagues who I worked with to define the Serving Salesperson concept discussed how could we integrate this point into the Seven Pillars. We knew we wanted our salespeople to be sincere givers who would focus their efforts on serving their customers and not allow themselves to be distracted by other activities. Paul, what does it mean to be *devoted* to something?"

"Well, the first word that comes to mind is *commitment*—that a person consistently dedicates their time, effort, and resources to the thing they are devoted to. I also think of being *loyal*—being faithful and supportive." Paul thought for a minute longer. "And sacrifice," he said. "That you are willing to give up other opportunities and maybe even experience some discomfort to make what you're devoted to your priority."

"It sounds like you were part of our discussion," said Matthew with a smile. "We concluded that a Serving Salesperson needs to be a *Devoted Giver*—devoted to creating an overwhelmingly positive and exceptionally satisfying experience for their customer. The Serving Salesperson is driven by a commitment and loyalty to serving their customers. They will even sacrifice their time and resources to serve the best interests of their customers and the relevant stakeholders that will be affected. Their level of devotion to their customers is selfless and goes above and beyond what's considered typical salesperson behavior."

Matthew continued, "As we said earlier, acting differently requires thinking differently. When you set serving as your true north, you'll find that assuming the role of a devoted giver will follow. When you served your customer by going to their plant to help meet their customer's delivery deadline, that is being a devoted giver. When you act in the best interests of others rather than yourself, you will gain a sense of satisfaction and fulfillment that's truly above and beyond."

Matthew continued, "By being a devoted giver a Serving Salesperson goes further than just meeting our customers' needs. Lew mentioned that when we live out the Seven Pillars in every interaction, we can transform the relationship with our customers and truly serve them. When customers believe we are genuinely there to serve, we earn the opportunity to guide them through their own transformation. We work to accomplish this by assisting them to realize that their aspirations are achievable, their obstacles are solvable, and their role as one of being empowered. Setting serving as your true north is the first step in transforming the relationship with your customer. As you go through your interviews with the TBS members they'll refer to how you can use the principles of their Pillar to continue to transform the relationship with your customers. As you might remember, the seventh Pillar is titled Guide the Transformation, and when you talk to John Philips, he'll bring all of this together for you.

"But if we become so focused on being devoted givers, won't there be people who see that as a sign of weakness and try to take advantage of you?" Paul asked. "How do you maintain your true north then?"

"Yes, unfortunately there will always be people who'll try to take advantage of you," answered Matthew. "But as a Serving Salesperson and a devoted giver our threshold for dealing with these types of customers is higher and goes above and beyond what other salespeople would be willing to deal with. However, while you are devoted to going above and beyond in serving your customer, sometimes you will reach a point when sacrificing your and your company's best interest can no longer be justified and it's untenable to continue."

"Now, let me take this in another direction," Matthew said. "We're talking about you making some significant changes in your life, and that isn't going to happen overnight. Throughout all your scheduled interviews you're going to have to prioritize your activities to be able to spend enough time to learn all the Pillars of being a Serving Salesperson."

Matthew paused and looked straight at Paul. "How productive are you in spending your time now?" he asked.

An Invitation

Paul was now totally drawn into the conversation. He was beginning to realize that not only was he getting the information he needed to satisfy Lew, but he was also getting some good ideas to make himself more productive, to make more sales and look better for the VP job.

Paul looked down, thinking about how he spent his time. During the week he was usually up around 5:30 a.m. to go to the fitness center, exercise, shower, grab a quick breakfast, and be at the office around 7:30. He would work until around 7:00 or 8:00 in the evening, largely because he didn't want to spend any more time alone in his empty apartment than he had to. On weekends when he didn't have his girls, he would usually go back to the office mainly to occupy himself so he wouldn't constantly be reminded that he had virtually no life outside of his work. He also thought about his recent travels, of sitting in hotel lounges talking with other salespeople who often were as lonely and rudderless as he was. He also thought of how the female servers seemed to get more attractive with each drink and how he would sometimes find himself having less than honorable thoughts about them. He shook his head to get back to the reality of the moment.

He looked up to find Matthew gazing intently at him. "I strongly encourage you to compose a personal mission statement," Matthew said. "That will be a great first step in transforming your mind into a true north mentality. You really need to take some time to think about what your personal mission should be and the direction you'd like your life to take."

"I'd like to do that, Matthew, but I wouldn't know how to go about it," he said, hoping that would give him the out he needed.

"I figured that would be the case, so I'd like to help you with that," Matthew said with a smile. He walked over to a table in the corner of his office and picked up a small box. Handing it to Paul, he said, "Inside are the keys to my lake cabin about an hour north of here in a little town called Pines Lake. There's also a map of how to get there as sometimes it doesn't come up on your phone. Lew and I thought it would be a good idea for you to go up there this weekend and conduct your own personal retreat.

"In this box are some reading materials and a few exercises on how to develop your own personal mission statement. I've included my statement to use as a guide, and be sure to take your journal and your computer as you'll be asked to record your thoughts as you go through these exercises."

Oh man, what have I gotten myself into? thought Paul.

"It looks like we'll have unusually good weather this weekend," Matthew continued, "so that won't be an issue. There are a few basic supplies at the cabin, but you may want to pick up a few food items at the general store there in Pines Lake just before you turn down the road to our cabin. Paul, there's no wi-fi, no TV, no radio, and you'll have to go back down to the main road to get reception for your cell phone. We want you to really focus on developing your personal mission statement."

Sitting back down, Matthew continued, "When you need a break, you can explore the property. My cabin sits on a lake, and I think you'll find there's a peace and a serenity in being there. If you allow yourself to be fully engaged in the exercises, you won't really want to talk to anyone else. I also think you'll learn that the more you get into the readings, you really will want to take the time to think about how you can begin to set serving as your true north."

Paul thought for a minute. He didn't have his girls this weekend, and besides, spending time by himself at a lake house would be a nice change from being cooped up in his office or alone in his apartment.

"That's very kind of you, Matthew. This sounds like it would be a good exercise to help me get more focused," Paul said, trying to sound convincing. He wasn't sure he pulled it off.

A Personal Retreat

On Friday afternoon he loaded his car, punched the address into his phone, and headed north on Route 33 to Pines Lake. He started thinking about how he was going to go about the task at hand. *I'm going to take the same approach to writing this mission statement as I did when I had to write a term paper in college. I'll learn just enough to get a good grade, pound out the paper, and hand it in. That should be good enough.*

Winding his way through the serene rural setting he found himself beginning to unwind and relax in a way he rarely felt anymore in his life. The road turned from two lanes to one lane, to gravel, and finally to dirt. After about a half mile on the wooded dirt road, the woods opened up into a two-acre clearing. He had arrived.

The cabin was a modern, one-story frame structure with a front porch big enough for four rocking chairs that faced a private lake of about fifteen acres. A dock extended into the lake with a beached canoe on one side and an aluminum rowboat on the other. There were no other houses on the lake. The rest of the seventy acres Matthew owned were designated as a tree farm.

Paul got out of the car and walked past a small fire pit ringed by logs for seating. He realized there was something different about this place, something he wasn't used to, something he couldn't put his finger on right away. After a moment he realized what it was.

It was the quiet.

The only sounds were the leaves rustling in the wind, the gentle lapping of waves on the shore, and a few birds singing in the trees. The serenity of the setting was more evident now. He found it incredibly soothing and paused for a few moments to take it all in.

Matthew was right, he thought.

He walked up to the cabin and let himself in. The cabin itself was small but comfortable, with a great room, kitchen, two bedrooms, a bathroom, laundry room, and a sleeping loft for children over the kitchen. The table to which Matthew referred sat in front of a large picture window with a stunning view of the lake. On the table were several books having to do with serving in one form or another along with a Bible. He opened the box and on the top of the pile found a reading list telling him what he was to read along with some simple instructions:

> Read the passage
> Reflect on its meaning
> Listen to your heart
> Journal your thoughts

The weather was indeed unseasonably warm for November. After settling in, Paul decided to take a walk and found a path through the pine trees. He had always found walking outside helped him feel more relaxed and creative.

When he returned to the cabin, he made himself a cup of coffee and picked up the first assignment on the reading list. He found it easy to get lost in what he was doing. He read and journaled his thoughts into the night, stopping only to heat up the pizza he had purchased at the general store. While he still wanted to just pound out the project, he was starting to see the benefit of some of what he was reading.

He became so engrossed in the readings and exercises that when he looked at his watch he was surprised when it was nearly midnight. He turned off the light, settled into bed, and was quickly serenaded to sleep by the sounds of crickets.

In the morning, he woke to the chirping of birds. After a short walk around the lake, he took out his computer, opened the workbook, and sat with the next reading assignment, occasionally looking up at the lake out the window. He read, reflected, and journaled throughout the morning and into the afternoon, pausing only for a quick lunch. He was surprised that not only was all of this going to help him write his personal mission statement, but he was realizing that he was enjoying the process.

Becoming a Serving Salesperson, however, was still too much of a stretch for him.

A Defining Moment

Later in the afternoon one of the readings contained the sentence: "What will people say about you at your funeral?"

That stopped him cold.

He stared out at the lake for a long time. He tried to get back to his reading, but the hamster wheel spinning in his mind wouldn't let him. The more he thought about it, the more unsettled he became. He wondered if he passed away suddenly, what would happen at his funeral? What would people say? His wife? His kids? His friends? His business associates? Would it be what he would want?

Then he remembered what Lew had told him. The salespeople who had adopted the Serving Salesperson mindset had not only changed the way they sell, but also how they approach their life.

Paul suddenly realized that he was now at a crossroads, at a defining moment in his life. What path was he going to take from here? This defining moment was not only going to impact his career but also his relationships with his family, customers, coworkers, friends, literally everyone he encountered. He now understood why Matthew was so insistent on him doing this personal retreat to look deep inside himself. He also realized that both Lew and Matthew wanted him to understand how becoming a Serving Salesperson could assist him in not only becoming a better salesperson but in becoming the type of person he really wanted to be.

Is this really happening? Surely not. I don't see myself being a servant to my customers. Let's get back to the task at hand.

Try as he might, it didn't work.

He continued to think about what he would want people to say about him at his funeral and what things needed to change in his life to make that happen. His brain was still spinning as he got into bed.

Surely this will pass, and I'll be my same old self in the morning, he thought, as he finally drifted off to sleep.

A New Mindset?

In the morning Paul woke up with the same feeling he had had the night before. He began to think to himself, *Why have I been so consumed with work, with getting more?* He realized that Mary was right—he really had been minimizing his time with her and his daughters, treating them more as distractions and seeking to limit his time with them so he could get back to the things he thought should be his priority.

He also realized that by being totally self-absorbed in his own priorities he had begun to view his coworkers as either tools to get what he wanted or as distractions to be minimized. He shook his head as he thought how he must have made his coworkers feel. *No wonder nobody likes me. Wow! I now see that composing this personal mission statement really needs to be more than simply a task to be done. Maybe, just maybe, it can help me set the internal compass to chart my path forward.*

As the afternoon began to turn into evening and it was approaching the time to head back, he perused his mission statement. While it was almost there, he wasn't quite satisfied with it. He needed an opening statement, something that really captured the essence of his personal mission. He just hadn't been quite able to put his finger on it.

While on Friday he had dreaded the drive and the task facing him, he was now almost reluctant to leave the serenity of Pines Lake. However, he was not at all sure how he was going to proceed when he got back. His talk with Matthew combined with his reflective weekend had made him realize that things had to change. He just wasn't sure how or what that would look like.

And then there was this Serving Salesperson thing. While a lot of the information he had read and included in his mission statement were reflective of serving his customer, for him to become a true Serving Salesperson still seemed a bridge too far. He could see himself being more customer focused, maybe working a bit harder for his customers, but being a Serving Salesperson the way Matthew described it? That just wasn't the way he was wired.

Back with Matthew

Monday morning Paul was back in Matthew's office returning the books and keys to his cabin. "It was truly wonderful, and I can't thank you enough for allowing me the privilege of doing that personal retreat and also giving me the direction you did," said Paul, finding it easier to mirror Matthew's kind countenance.

"I only set the table for you. It was you who did all the work and realized that your internal compass needed adjusting," Matthew replied. "Now, I'd like to give you more of a sense of what it's like to really serve others. Are you aware of the outreach project the men's ministry at church is doing this coming weekend?"

Paul shook his head.

Matthew continued, "The church has a partnership with Horizon House, a shelter for women and children who are victims of domestic violence. About a year ago, Horizon House was able to purchase an old apartment building, and the men's ministry has been helping to rehab it. We will be there again this weekend to complete the rehab so women and their children who have a need can come there to escape their situation. Why don't you come and work on it this weekend, Paul? You'll really get a taste of what it means to truly serve others."

"I'd like to come, but I have my girls this weekend."

So much the better. Many of the guys bring their kids as well. The guys who have brought their kids found it to be a great bonding experience, plus it's also a great way to get your children thinking about serving."

Paul remembered that the girls were always talking about wanting to do something different on their weekends with him. He also thought it might provide him the insights he needed to begin to adopt a Serving Salesperson mindset.

"I'll, I mean, we'll, do it" said Paul, "What time should we be there?"

"Breakfast is at 8:00 and we start work at 8:30. Come and I guarantee when you see what we can accomplish, you'll discover the true joy of serving others."

Serving and Learning

Paul rousted Elizabeth and Ruthie out of bed at his apartment on Saturday morning and headed over to Horizon House. The weekend activities were unlike anything Paul had ever experienced. Around fifty men along with a couple dozen of their children of all ages descended on the apartment building and were diligently working as well as any professional crew.

The thing that really struck him, however, was the serving attitude of everyone he encountered. Here were men from all walks of life, with all different skill levels, all there for the purpose of doing something for someone else—and doing so with a joyful attitude.

Paul's girls, while a bit hesitant at first, quickly pitched in and took to their assigned tasks with gusto. They returned on Sunday, and by Sunday evening the fifteen apartments were totally reconfigured to accommodate the families that needed them. The deadline to finish was 6:00 p.m., as that was when the board of directors of Horizon House was coming to view what they had accomplished.

As the board members began to arrive, Paul felt a tap on his shoulder. He turned to find Matthew behind him. "A family is coming in shortly. I don't know much about them—only that it is an emergency situation, and they needed housing immediately. I thought that you might want to give the girls the experience."

"Of course," Paul said. He felt this would be a good teaching moment for his girls, an object lesson about helping others. Little did he know that it would be a teaching moment for him.

As some of the men left, a caravan of trucks and vans pulled up with food, personal items, and furniture for the apartments. A group of women who Paul learned were from the women's ministry at the church and the men who remained behind began unloading furniture, making beds, and stocking shelves in anticipation of the arrival of the new residents.

It didn't take long.

A True Serving Experience

If you didn't know there was a family coming in you wouldn't have noticed. A mother and two girls about the same age as Elizabeth and Ruthie walked silently and very tentatively into the shelter. The mother had a vacant expression and didn't seem aware that her girls were both clinging to her. The younger one was holding a fluffy pink bear tight to her chest. Each girl was carrying a large plastic trash bag.

"Daddy, they look scared," Ruthie whispered to Paul.

They did indeed look scared. *Shell shocked*, Paul thought to himself. Even though she had tried to cover it with makeup, Paul could make out a bruise on the mother's cheek.

Paul then heard Ruthie gently say to the littlest girl, "Here, can I show you your room?"

She looked up at her mother for approval.

Still with a vacant expression, her mother gave her a silent nod.

Ruthie took her hand. "My name's Ruthie. What's yours?"

The girl mumbled, "Brianna."

Ruthie took Brianna's hand and together they walked into one of the bedrooms. Then it was Elizabeth's turn to take after her sister.

"Would you like to see your room too? I'm Elizabeth," she said to the older girl. "What's your name?"

The older girl, while still clearly unsure of what to do, mumbled, "Jasmine," and then asked, "Can I go too, Mama?"

Another silent nod. Elizabeth and Jasmine followed Ruthie and Brianna into the girls' bedroom. Paul could hear Ruthie ask, "What's your bear's name?"

"Pink Bear."

"Can I pet him?"

Brianna must have said yes because Paul heard Ruthie say, "He's really soft. When you hold him, does it make you feel better?"

"Yes," came the weak reply.

"Well, I have someone who makes me feel better too. It's an otter named Ollie. When I was little and felt sad, he always made me feel better. Well, let's see what we can do to make Pink Bear feel at home. Where do you think he would like to sleep?"

That broke the ice, and soon Paul's daughters were talking with the other girls about things girls their age talk about—pop stars, music videos, social media, how boys are mostly stupid, and so forth.

Paul watched silently, wiping some tears off his cheek.

"Serving can take many forms." He had not heard Matthew come up behind him. "Setting serving as your true north does not only apply to our jobs," Matthew said gently, "it applies to the way we live, to the way we behave toward others."

Paul suddenly felt moved to speak. "I'd like to learn how to serve others better, but I wouldn't know where to begin," he said, his voice cracking.

Matthew looked at him and said softly, "You begin with a choice."

You begin with a choice.

The ride home started quietly. After a couple of minutes Paul spoke up. "What you two did for those two girls was really special. What made you think to do that?" In the rearview mirror he could see the girls looking at each other.

Ruthie spoke up first. "In Sunday school our teacher is always saying that we need to look for ways to help others when they need it," she said. "All the time she reminds us of the golden rule: Do to others as you would have them do to you."

Elizabeth piped up. "Jasmine was really afraid," she said. "She said they had seen some really scary things. I just saw someone who needed a friend."

Ruthie chimed in. "Brianna and I are the same age, and she was scared too. My Sunday school teacher also says to try to look for ways to help others, to practice the golden rule. I just tried to treat Brianna the way I would want to be treated if the same thing had happened to me."

A huge light bulb went on in Paul's head. Here he had been struggling to find some sort of pathway to adopt the Serving Salesperson's mindset, and his daughters had just given it to him. The golden rule—treat others the way you would want to be treated. It was so simple yet so profound. Here he thought that staying behind would be a teaching moment for his girls, but he ended up being the one learning the lesson. Matthew's words came back to him.

You begin with a choice.

After driving in silence for a while Elizabeth spoke up. "That was really neat, Dad," she said, "thanks for asking us to help you. Can you come in so we can tell Mom about it?" Paul didn't usually come in when he dropped the girls off, but since they asked, he would oblige.

The girls burst into the house. "Mom! It was sooo cool!" The girls said in unison. "We really had a great time, and we got to meet and help one of the families get settled in. And Dad was awesome!" Mary gave Paul a quizzical look, as she wasn't used to the girls calling him awesome.

"I was really proud of them," Paul said, "and you would have been really proud of them too."

Paul and Mary suffered then through a few seconds of awkward silence, which was mercifully broken when Elizabeth said, "Did you get those new dresses of ours finished, Mom?"

"Yes, I did," answered Mary "Why don't you run upstairs and try them on?" With squeals of delight, the girls bounded upstairs. As they reached the top of the stairs, Elizabeth turned around and called out, "Thanks again, Dad; it really was *awesome!*"

"I guess you made quite an impression on them," Mary said softly, the kind of tone she used to have before the fighting began. Paul hadn't heard her speak to him in that tone for a long time. He realized how much he had missed it.

"It was really, well, fulfilling, Mary, serving others," Paul began, and before he knew it, he was telling her all about this time with

Matthew, his personal retreat, writing his mission statement, and the experience at the shelter. Mary listened with a suspicious look on her face, as she'd heard the "I'm really going to change this time" speech before. Paul wanted to tell her more about what the girls had done, but she cut him off.

"Well," she said, assuming what had become her usual dismissive tone, "I really do hope that talking with all these people of—what did you say, the TBS? —will change the way you look at things. Maybe it will make you want to work on our marriage more than you have. That was not an idle threat I gave you. If you're not going to work on solving the problems in our marriage, I'm going to move forward. Now, if you'll excuse me, I must make sure the girls are cleaned up and are ready for school tomorrow."

The Mission Statement

Back at his apartment Paul collapsed into a chair with a feeling that he hadn't had in a long time—maybe ever. He thought about his meeting with Matthew, his time at the lake, what people would say at his funeral, the weekend service project, and what Ruthie had said to him. Since returning from the lake he had been searching for some insight that would lead him to adopting the Serving Salesperson mindset. And then he thought of two statements.

You begin with a choice and *do to others as you would have them do to you.*

Here he had spent last couple of days trying to come up with some earth-shattering, dramatic thought to begin his mission statement, and in just a few minutes at the shelter it had all come into focus for him. Rather than trying to adopt some sort of grandiose statement to impress Matthew and Lew, he realized what he needed to focus on was making the choice to treat others the way he would want to be treated. Sure, it was going to take some effort; he would have to reorient the way he approached others. But it was not a complicated, involving process. He just had to imagine himself in the other person's shoes and think how he would want to be treated. Then he should choose to treat that person in that exact same way—doing unto them as he would have them do to him.

Paul realized that he found himself thinking differently—like the renewing of his mind that both Lew and Matthew had mentioned. He realized that serving others could give him a sense of fulfillment, and that by living by the golden rule he truly could help others reach their desired goals. Suddenly, a thought struck him, and he hurried to his computer, opened his personal mission statement file, and began typing these words: *To make a difference in people's lives for the better by discovering and serving their needs.*

That was it—his primary purpose. If he could be true to this statement, it would change the way he looked at the world and help him to serve others and treat them the way he would want to be treated. This was a true paradigm shift for him. He knew it was one he should make, one he *had* to make. The feeling he was beginning to have was unlike anything he had ever experienced, and he wanted to keep it going, to have those feelings all the time, to embed them into the very essence of his being.

And, Paul thought, *working to serve my customers should help me get the VP job at the same time. It's a win-win!*

Thinking Differently

At the end of the month Paul was back in Matthew's office, showing him his journal, his mission statement, and all the exercises he completed. Matthew smiled as he read Paul's mission statement, especially the first sentence about seeking to serve others. After some time, Matthew looked up and said, "So, what have you learned about setting serving as your true north?"

"What you told me at the shelter—you begin with a choice—has had a profound effect on me," Paul replied. "It has helped me to *choose* to serve others and really think about how I can meet their needs rather than concentrating on my own. I've also noticed that when I began to think about how to best serve my customers, I acted differently. I must confess I don't totally understand the entire Serving Salesperson mindset yet, but I'm going to continue to work on it. What I have realized is that if you choose to live by the golden rule, you not only will help your customers, but it's so much more rewarding than just trying to gain things for yourself. I've also learned that they'll be much more open and honest with you, which leads to opportunities that weren't there when you walked in."

As Matthew listened to Paul, even he was amazed at the change he'd seen in the past month. He looked up with a big smile and said, "It really appears that you're well on your way of setting your true north around serving the customer. You just need to continue to be transformed by the renewing of your mind, and when your mind is transformed, you'll learn more about how to transform the relationship with your customers. As it says in Second Corinthians 9:7, 'Each of you should give what you have decided in your heart to give, not reluctantly or under compulsion.' I feel you're ready to move on to the next Pillar: Blend Passion and Perseverance, and I know that Martha Peters is waiting to talk to you. I've enjoyed our time together, Paul, and I especially enjoyed watching you embrace the first Pillar of Set Serving as Your True North.

"Well done!"

Blend Passion and Perseverance

Grit is that "extra something" that separates the most successful people from the rest. It's the passion, perseverance, and stamina that we must channel in order to stick with our dreams until they become a reality.

—*Travis Bradberry*

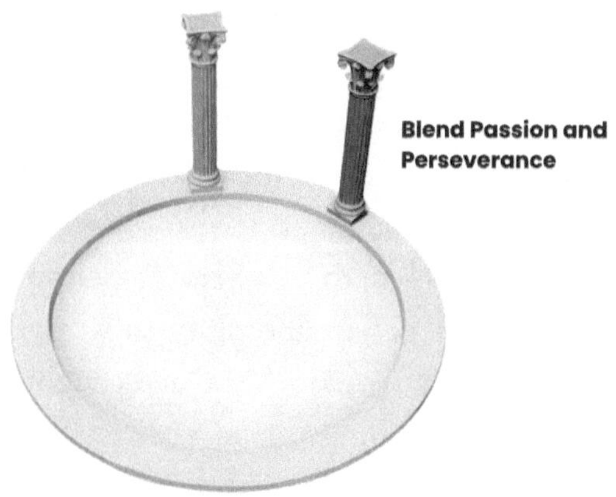

Coming in Hot

PAUL NOW FOUND himself looking at the world through a different lens. Talking with Matthew, the weekend at the lake house, and participating in the Horizon House project had been an epiphany for him. He was beginning to think differently as well. The first sentence of his mission statement—*To make a difference in people's lives for the better by discovering and serving their needs*—was becoming his new mindset. He felt that this new serving mindset could help him get the increased sales he needed to get the VP job, but he was still trying to figure it all out.

A week or so later on a chilly December morning Paul was driving to the offices of Martha Peters, the president of a management recruiting firm. Martha's team had won several awards from their national corporation and had quite a few glowing reviews from previous clients.

Paul was ushered back to Martha's office where she greeted him warmly. Martha, a jovial grandmotherly type in her sixties clasped his hand with both of hers, which immediately made him feel comfortable. "Come in, Paul," she said with a big smile. "I had a nice conversation with Matthew Solomon the other day about your progress with the first Pillar." She walked to a chair at her round conference table, sat down, and invited Paul to do the same. "Now," she said, settling in across from Paul, "tell me what you've learned so far about being a Serving Salesperson."

When Paul had finished telling Martha everything he had learned so far, she responded with a warm smile. "It sounds like Matthew has worked his usual magic with you, and it also sounds like you're beginning to understand what it's like to be a Serving Salesperson." Suddenly Martha leaned forward in her chair and practically barked at Paul, "Tell me, Paul, why do you do what you do?" She had caught Paul completely off guard, and he began searching for an answer. Before he could respond she followed up with barking another question: "And what do you do when you get knocked down and don't want to get back up?"

After a few seconds of silently staring at him sternly, Martha just as quickly changed back into the charming person that had greeted him. "I'm sorry to have come in hot there, Paul," she said with a warm smile, "but I've found that's a good way to get people thinking about the second Pillar of being a Serving Salesperson: Blend Passion and Perseverance. Why don't you relax and let's talk about the importance of this Pillar?

"As you've experienced, a salesperson's road is never straight," she began, sounding a lot like Matthew with her educational tone. "It's a winding, crooked path full of ups and downs, twists and turns. That's why you need to begin with Set Serving as Your True North. So, Paul, how do you think successful salespeople grind through all of these obstacles, day after day?"

Paul thought for a moment. "Well," he said, "I've found that most of the time you just have to keep your head down and focus on plowing through until you're able to close the deal."

"You're on the right track there, Paul, but we need to tweak that a bit. Researchers have found a formula for achieving success in sales that is better than any combination of talent, luck, or fate. And that something is grit. When someone says, 'You have to have grit,' what does that mean to you?"

Grinding Through

Paul thought for a minute and responded, "I see grit as being willing to tough it out through whatever roadblocks and setbacks you encounter during the sales process."

"That's certainly an important part of sales," Martha answered, "And this falls right in line with being the Devoted Giver that Matthew talked about. A Devoted Giver has a passion for serving their customer. In addition to having a passion for serving, Serving Salespeople also must exhibit perseverance and motivation despite all the failures and adversity that comes with being a salesperson. These two factors come together to form the second Pillar of being a Serving Salesperson: Blend Passion and Perseverance."

> *A serving salesperson must have the passion and exhibit perseverance to serve their customer*

"I can see how perseverance fits in," said Paul. "But what part does passion play?"

"Passion is the character trait that motivates and sustains you," Martha replied. "First you set serving as your true north. But being a

Serving Salesperson goes further. There must also be a passion to serve your customers. When you have a true passion for something, it's the last thing you think about when you're going to sleep and the first thing you think about when you wake up."

Paul thought wistfully back to the time when he first started out in sales. He was young, enthusiastic, and passionate about almost everything—his job, serving his customers, his marriage to his college sweetheart, being a husband and then a father. He remembered leaping out of bed in the morning excited to face the day. He realized he hadn't felt that way in a long time, and he also realized how much he missed it.

Martha asked him gently, "Why do you suppose you don't feel that way anymore?"

It's like she's reading my mind, Paul thought. He already knew the answer and said, "It wasn't a sudden change. It just sort of crept in, and it seemed like whatever I had wasn't enough. I wanted more. And you know what? When I got those commissions, bonuses, and promotions, they didn't bring me anywhere near the satisfaction I thought they would. I know I've gotten off track, and I'd love to get that passion back."

"That's why we're both here," Martha replied softly.

Regaining Passion

"I'm assuming you have written a personal mission statement?" Martha asked.

"Yes."

"Can you tell me the essence of what that statement says?"

"Here, let me show you," said Paul, handing it to her.

"To make a difference in people's lives for the better by discovering and serving their needs," Martha read aloud, and a smile crossed her face. "This is excellent, Paul. The first sentence of your mission statement can serve as a starting point for regaining your passion.

"Paul, successful people set an overarching, long-term goal not just for what they want to accomplish in the short term but into the future as well. Focusing on an overarching goal inspires you to develop a passion to achieve that goal. That goal becomes your ultimate concern and helps you determine the day-to-day goals you want to achieve. Meeting those day-to-day goals allows you to work your way up to meeting your overarching goal.

Successful people set an overarching, long-term goal that inspires them to develop a passion to achieve that goal.

"The first sentence from your mission statement that you just showed me tells me your overarching goal. What does this mean to you, Paul?"

Paul leaned back in his chair and began to ruminate with a faraway look in his eyes. "It shows me what my passion, my personal philosophy, what that *thing* that drives me should be," he said. "I see now why Matthew was so insistent that I write a personal mission statement."

Martha smiled a knowing smile. "Gritty people first establish their overarching goal and then hold that same goal for a very long time. That goal becomes their life philosophy and is so interesting and so intense for them that it organizes a great deal of their waking activity. For gritty people, their daily goals are, in some way, related to meeting their overarching goal. The more you focus on achieving these goals, the more focused your passion becomes."

"Wow, Martha, the answer to getting my passion back was literally right in front of me. I just didn't put it all together until now."

"Now you're also coming to the realization of what it truly means to be a Serving Salesperson, Paul. When you have that first Pillar of serving your customers as your overarching goal, you have the beginning of your framework for developing that passion to serve. "That's a lot to take in in such a short time. I think we could both use a break to let all this sink in for a few minutes," she said, "May I refresh your coffee for you?"

Achieving Results

After a few minutes with fresh cups of coffee Martha asked, "Paul, did you participate in athletics in school?"

"Yes, I was a swimmer in high school and college."

"I ran cross-country in high school and college, and I remember those long practice runs. Running cross-country has a lot of similarities to being a swimmer. So, was it *fun* training to be a competitive swimmer, like playing golf or tennis is fun?"

Paul laughed. "You should know the answer to that, Martha. There's nothing much fun about going up and down the pool a few hundred times a workout."

"And would you say you were the most talented swimmer on the team?"

"I was pretty good, but in both high school and college there were guys who were better than me."

"So, if swim workouts weren't much fun and you were competing with guys who had more talent than you, how did you get through those workouts?"

After thinking for a moment, Paul spoke up. "You just have to make yourself do it. You have to say to yourself, 'I want to get better; I want to lower my times.' The only way you were going to get better was to keep pushing through even though sometimes you just wanted to quit. I knew that I had to make up for my lack of natural talent by working harder than everyone else. And it worked. I lettered all four years in college and my senior year I was voted captain of the swim team."

Martha leaned back in her chair and paused. "So, you had to persevere."

"Ah, I see where this is going," Paul answered. "We're going to talk about the second part of having grit—perseverance."

"That's right," said Martha. "Having the talent to do something is important to getting results. But effort figures in there as well. In fact, it figures in a lot. When you put forth the effort, you develop skills.

And then when you combine those skills with effort, you achieve results. What stands out to you about that?"

> *When you put forth the effort, you develop skills. When combining those skills with effort you achieve results.*

"I notice that effort factors into achieving results not once, but twice," Paul said.

Martha nodded and said, "Having talent is one thing. But putting forth the effort to develop that talent is quite another. We both have known people who have had talent in a certain area but did not put forth the effort required to reach their full potential. And we also know people who may not have been the most talented but did put forth the effort and were able to achieve the results they wanted.

"Gritty salespeople do the same thing. They persevere through the long days and evenings of toil that the job requires. They persevere through the longer sales cycles and the increased complexities of the customer's purchase journey. If you put in the effort, Paul, you'll find there are no traffic jams on the extra mile.

"There's one other thing to mention here, Paul. A Serving Salesperson is always looking for ways to transform the relationship with our customers. That is not something that is going to happen in one or even a few interactions with them. Once you have set serving as your true north, the next step in transforming the relationship is exhibiting the passion the perseverance to continue that mindset consistently throughout your time with the customer.

"You've given me a lot to think about, Martha, and I really want to become grittier. Other than my own efforts, can you recommend any other things I might do to become grittier?"

"A big help in becoming grittier is to find a gritty culture with gritty people and join it. A key to becoming gritty is to surround yourself with people who are like-minded, who will inspire you and bring you up to their level."

That made Paul wince. He thought about the guys he had been hanging around with, particularly those since his separation from Mary. They weren't exactly a who's who of the most credible characters you'd want to meet. He thought about something his saintly grandmother always used to tell him: If you put on a white glove and go out and play in the mud, the mud doesn't get glovey.

"You live up or down as a result of the people you surround yourself with, so you need to decide who those people are going to be." Martha continued, "Who might be some people that you would consider gritty who you could meet with as sort of a mutual pumping-up society?"

Regaining Grit

Paul immediately thought of two people at Petra—Cathy Perkins and Ed Fetter. Both had grit, that combination of passion and perseverance that made them successful salespeople. When he first met Cathy and Ed early on in his time with Petra, he knew they would be great role models. He pulled out his phone and immediately made a note to himself to call them after finishing his meeting with Martha.

Martha again leaned forward to emphasize her next point. "Paul, you must realize that while others can help you, *you* are the only one who can do this. Your mission statement becomes your motivation to move forward. You then need to think about *how* you're going to move forward and what tools, resources, and assets you need to bring to the table to make it happen. You've got your mission statement, and some of this you'll learn from the other members of the TBS. But ultimately it must come from deep inside you."

Martha flipped over a couple of pages in Paul's journal. "As with setting your true north," she said, "your journal has some exercises to complete. I suggest you set aside several hours over the next week first to go online to examine the resources provided on developing grit and then go through these exercises. Some of the exercises will require you to think about them on your own while others will involve taking a more active role at work. When you realize the resources that are available to you, I think you'll find you have a lot to be passionate about."

Paul looked down at the page entitled "Blend Passion and Perseverance Exercises" and found activities such as writing down his goals and then determining how they led up to his overarching goal, documenting how he handled negative experiences, and other exercises to build mental strength and endurance. He realized that he had never done any of these and could see how they could help ignite the passion for his job.

Martha continued, "As you work through these exercises, I think you'll be pleasantly surprised at the impact they can have. We all want to do our best, and I really think you just need to refocus your energies on those avenues that will help you blend passion and perseverance to help you achieve your overarching goal of serving your customers and transforming your relationship with them.

"So, have you got enough to keep you busy for a while?" she asked with a beaming smile.

"Wow, I sure do, Martha. I can't thank you enough for your time, and especially for your insight. You've given me a lot to think about."

"It's been a pleasure to meet you and talk with you, Paul," said Martha, extending her hand. "I look forward to hearing back from you at the end of the month."

Paul sat in his car in the parking lot for a few minutes before heading out. *If I can recapture the passion I had when I first started out in sales, I really think I can get back to where I need to be both at work and maybe even at home,* he thought. *Then I must have the perseverance to see all of this through. That would also help me to position myself for the VP job.*

Paul scrolled through his contact list and punched a number. After two rings he heard, "Cathy Perkins."

"Hi, Cathy, it's Paul. I have a favor to ask of you."

Having Lunch

Three days later Paul was sitting at lunch with Cathy and Ed. "We're curious as to why you wanted to meet with us after such a long time," Ed began slowly, choosing his words carefully while shooting a look at Cathy as the Walters Enterprise situation was common knowledge by now. "What's on your mind?"

Paul thought how a few short weeks ago he would have launched into a defensive tirade, insisting that his shortcoming was someone else's fault and positioning himself squarely as the victim. Instead, he paused for a minute and answered quietly, "I'm working on changing the way I look at the world, guys," he said, looking down at the table. "I want to have more of a serving mentality, and I wanted to talk to you guys about how you developed and have kept your passion for your job." He raised his head up and looked at both of them. "Can we talk about that?"

Both Cathy and Ed could not hide their surprised looks. They were totally unprepared for the quiet, purposeful, and humble demeanor they found in Paul. They sat in silence for a moment before Cathy finally spoke up.

"It comes from inside, Paul," she said, "from being a devoted giver and always wanting to do your best for your customers. What gives me my passion is that I love to do whatever I can to help my customers meet their needs. There's a different challenge every day, and there's always something to learn from each one. The longer I do this job, the more I can learn, and the more I'm prepared for those unusual situations that will inevitably come up. I've found that even in the simplest of situations I'll almost always learn something that I can file in my memory for use in another situation. And sooner rather than later I can use that information to help the next customer in new and different way."

Ed chimed in, "As I'm one of the old hands around here you could say that my priorities have changed. When I was younger, it was all about proving myself first to myself and then to those around me. The first job I had was in sales in Chicago, and I was determined not to let those big city boys beat my numbers. I worked extremely hard not to serve my customers but just to beat everyone else's numbers and get the recognition that came with it. However, I found that external rewards take you only so far. Now I get far more satisfaction from when the customer takes me aside, shakes my hand, and tells me they couldn't have accomplished what they've been able to without me. That's what keeps me going."

The one-hour lunch extended over with Paul getting Ed's and Cathy's insightful perspectives. He realized how positive both were and what a great influence they had been on his life at Petra and undoubtedly were on others' lives as well. He also realized how much he had missed spending time with them. He finally bid them goodbye but not before scheduling another lunch for a month hence.

Martha was right, Paul thought as he walked back to his office after thanking them and sending them on their way. *Spending time with positive people really does have an impact on your perspective.*

Paul spent the days after his meeting with Martha differently. While he had always been meticulous in using his calendar to plan how he was going to spend his days, he had given very little thought to prioritizing his second- or third-layer goals to make sure they helped him achieve his overarching goal of making a difference in people's lives for the better by discovering and serving their needs. Also, rather than having a pessimistic outlook on what he didn't have, he focused on having an optimistic outlook on the positive things in his life, the things he could be truly thankful for.

It wasn't long before Paul's commitment to serving the needs of one of his customers was put to the test.

Put to the Test

A few days later Paul received an urgent call from his sometime customer Neil Todd, who he referred to as that crusty old curmudgeon. Paul always left his meetings with Neil feeling like he had been drinking sour lemonade the whole time. Neil was the plant manager for a medium-sized manufacturing firm located to the north of Petra and only called Paul as a last resort. He was extremely difficult to deal with, being singularly focused on driving the price down as far as he could—and then some.

It turned out that Neil's plant was having an issue with one of the machines on their production line, and if it wasn't fixed, it would cause them to miss a customer's delivery deadline. He remembered Paul talking about a product that might fix the problem. He asked if Paul could come over and see if he could help.

Driving over to Neil's plant was just about the last thing Paul wanted to do. It was about an hour and a half drive with the last half of it being on a winding two-lane road. It had snowed the night before and it was beginning to snow again. Paul also knew when he got there, he was going to have to deal with that crusty old curmudgeon who would undoubtedly attempt to make his life more difficult. He really didn't want to go at all. However, he had detected more than a twinge of desperation in Neil's voice. Then he thought of Matthew's words to him at the shelter—*You begin with a choice.* He called Neil to tell him he was on his way and reluctantly climbed into his car and headed over to Neil's plant. The closer he got the more he dreaded the meeting. The roads were getting worse and even if his product could solve Neil's problem, he wasn't sure he wanted to deal with the aggravation. It began snowing a bit harder, and he knew if he was there for any length of time he'd have to drive home in the dark with more snow on the road. He decided it wasn't worth it; he was going to take the first opportunity to turn around and head home.

He turned into the first gas station he came to and turned his car around. As he turned his head to look for oncoming cars, however, his eyes fell upon the index card he had put on the dashboard with the first line of his mission statement: *To make a difference in people's lives for the better by discovering and serving their needs.* He thought about what that meant. Then he thought about Matthew's words. He took a deep breath and turned the steering wheel the other way.

A bit less than an hour later he was walking into Neil's plant.

"I'm surprised to see you," Neil exclaimed. "I thought with the roads being so nasty you'd have called me and canceled. You really must have had to stick to it to get here."

While on the surface Neil appeared to be his usual gruff and grumpy self, Paul could tell something was bothering him. As Neil described the problem the production line was having, Paul saw that he was clearly nervous about the problem. He knew that his product could fix it in a satisfactory manner, and if the problem was as bad as Neil said it would be one of the big sales that Paul needed to chalk up for the VP job. However, he also knew that Precision Products, Paul's main competitor, had a product that would be better suited to provide a solution to Neil's problem than Petra's would be. It was apparent that Neil did not know about Precision's product. Paul thought about what his next move should be, but not for very long.

The old Paul would have waxed eloquently about the virtues of his product, closed the sale immediately, and expedited the delivery before Neil could find out otherwise. The new Paul, however, thought about his mission statement, his overarching goal, and the best way to serve the customer. Then he thought about Ruthie's words about the golden rule. As Neil was talking Paul stopped him at mid-sentence.

"Neil, we can certainly offer a solution to the issue you're having," he said, "and it would be an adequate fix. However, Precision Products has the exact product you need, and it would be a much better solution to your problem, and I think might even positively transform your entire operation. Would you like me to call Bill Kelso, their salesperson, for you?"

Neil could only stare at Paul in stunned silence. He apparently could not believe what he was hearing. "You mean you—just about the most competitive guy that calls on me—would give up a big order just like that for me?"

Paul smiled and said, "Neil, my mission is to serve my customers to the best of my ability, and right now putting you in touch with Precision for this situation is the best way to do that. Let me get the process started."

Paul pulled out his phone, looked up Bill Kelso's number, and hit the call button. Bill answered after two rings with a curt, "What's up, Paul?" as they had had a couple of run-ins over some common customers.

Paul briefly explained Neil's situation and ended it with, "Let me hand you over to Neil and you guys can take it from there." He handed his phone to Neil and stepped outside the office.

After a few minutes Neil came out of his office and handed Paul his phone back. He had a big smile on his face. Paul was not sure he'd ever seen Neil smile before. His entire demeanor had changed from that crusty old curmudgeon to being downright pleasant. "Bill is coming over tomorrow, and you were right. The way he described how his product worked would be a better solution than your product and could indeed improve our operation. I still can't believe that you would do this for me, Paul. I don't think I've ever had a salesperson not only recommend a competitor's product but expedite it happening," Neil said, still smiling. "Come back into my office. I have something for you."

Paul followed Neil back into his office where Neil opened the door to a closet in the corner. He took out a bottle of wine and handed it to Paul. "I make this myself. It's sort of a hobby of mine. It's the gift I give out at Christmas for people I consider special, and I always make a few extra bottles for just such occasions. It's pretty good if I do say so myself, and it's my way of saying thank you." He gave Paul the bottle and a firm handshake. "I want you to let me know right away when you have any new products you think we'd be interested in. And Paul, you're going to be the first person I call next time I have an issue." Neil's phone rang. "Sorry, I need to take this. Thanks again, and you can go out that way," he said gesturing down the hall, "right past Ciaran's desk."

Paul walked toward the front door carrying his bottle of wine. As he passed Ciaran's desk, she casually looked up, and then immediately her head snapped back up with a wide-eyed look. "Wow!" she exclaimed, "What did *you* do to get one of his bottles of wine?! It must have been something *really* special!"

On the dark and rather slippery drive back home Paul reflected on what had just happened. He looked over at the bottle of wine on the front seat and smiled to himself. He felt as though he was really beginning to realize how much of an impact the first two Pillars of being a Serving Salesperson had had on him in such a short period of time. A few months ago, he wouldn't have given a second thought to immediately closing the order with Neil and congratulating himself on the big sale. Today, however, he didn't hesitate to take the steps that were the best way to serve his customer. Sure, he lost a sale in the short run, but he knew he had served his customer in the best way he knew how and felt confident that his actions would benefit Petra down the road. He felt rewarded in several ways.

A Verification

The next afternoon Paul's phone buzzed. It was Bill Kelso. "Hi, Paul," Bill said, "I just wanted to thank you for connecting me with Neil Todd. We were able to not only solve the problem he knew he had but a couple more pressing ones that he didn't know he had."

Then there was a short hesitation in the conversation.

"And there's one other thing," Bill began slowly. "Paul, for you to hand that sale over to me was totally unexpected, and, I have to say, not something I ever would have imagined you doing. But the way you reached out, your demeanor and the tone of our conversation, well, it seems that something has really changed about you. Neil and I talked about it as he noticed it too. He said that you told him something about your mission being to serve your customers, and Paul, you really exemplified it there. Neil is going to post your actions on social media and I'm going to as well. I don't know how you decided that serving your customers was going to be your mission but keep it up. It really suits you well."

After the call ended Paul sat back in his chair and let out a long sigh. A couple of months ago if he had lost a sale like that, he would have imagined a bird carrying a "VP of Sales" sign flying out the window. Now, with his new attitude about serving his customers and working to transform his relationship with them, he would go over, open the window, and watch the bird fly away. He really felt that he had been transformed by the renewing of his mind, just as Lew had said. Also, he had been thinking that the VP job was just not that important to him anymore, and the recent events solidified it for him. He realized he no longer wanted the position, the status, the additional authority, and the extra money that came with it. His time at the lake house, the events at the Horizon House, the conversation with his girls in the car, and now his experience with Neil Todd's company brought two statements into his mind:

You begin with a choice.

Do to others as you would have them do to you.

Yes, being a Serving Salesperson really does suit me, Paul thought to himself. *And not only does it suit me, it's also what I want to do, the direction I want to take. Serving others has given me much more satisfaction than I ever thought it would. By serving others I truly can live out my mission statement and make a difference in people's lives for the better. That's the road I'm going to travel from here on.*

Dealing with Christmas

As Christmas approached, Paul began to think how he would handle things with his family. This would be the first Christmas since he had moved out, and he knew that Mary was still angry and hurt by his actions. Mary was taking the girls to her parents' house out of state for the holidays, and he had made plans with some men he'd met on the Horizon House project to work Christmas Eve and Christmas Day serving dinner at a soup kitchen. However, he knew he couldn't just let the holiday pass. He knew he was wrong in moving out, and he desperately wanted to try and patch things up with Mary. He also knew he had hurt her deeply, and it was going to take time and more proactive action on his part to show her he had truly changed. He knew that it would be up to him to take the first step. He took out his phone and hit her number.

"Hello," she said, icily.

"Hi, it's me. Are you still going to your parents' house for Christmas?"

"Yes," said Mary coolly.

"Before you go, I'd like to get the girls something special for Christmas. They've been talking about wanting cell phones. Would it be okay with you if I got each of them one?"

"I can't afford that, Paul. You know I'm only working part-time."

"I know you can't. How about if I put them on our plan and also pay for it? That way you won't have any added expense, and—"

"And what?" Mary interrupted, sounding impatient.

"I'd just like to help out more than I've been doing."

"That's nice of you," Mary said, her voice softening a bit.

"If it's okay with you," Paul said, "when I pick them up this Friday, we'll go to the phone store. I'll let them pick one out—within reason of course," he said with a laugh.

Silence on the other end of the phone.

"We'll have our own little Christmas celebration when I drop them off on Sunday before you head out the next day. And ...." his voice trailed off as he was searching for what to say next.

"And what?" said Mary, again sounding impatient.

"I'm sorry. I'm sorry for how I've hurt you, and I hope I can show you that I've changed, that I want to work on our marriage, and that someday you'll forgive me. And I hope you have a great Christmas with your parents, and I'll miss being with all of you."

Again, silence on the other end of the phone. Finally, Mary spoke. "That would be nice, and I'll see you Friday." Paul thought he detected a softening in her voice.

Putting Grit into Practice

Just before New Year's Paul was once again sitting in Martha's office, watching as she read over his journal and nodded approvingly. "So, how do you feel about your job now?" she asked.

"The more I set about trying to practice making a difference in people's lives for the better by discovering and serving their needs, the more I realize how much I had forgotten how satisfying it is to not only serve the needs of your customer but also those around you as well. When Matthew Solomon talked about being a Devoted Giver, it really gave me something to think about. You were right, Martha, most salespeople really do like helping others, and I've really focused on serving my customers, helping them to meet their goals, and working to transform my relationship with them. I know that this is something that's not going to happen overnight, but I've noticed how differently customers react to me when I talk about meeting their needs, and get them thinking about how to do their business better."

"And how have things changed with your coworkers?" Martha asked.

Paul leaned forward and said enthusiastically, "I've also come to realize that I work for an incredible company with great colleagues, and associating with those colleagues who are passionate about serving their customers encourages me to do the same. I'm in a great situation, and now I can't wait to start every day. I guess you could say that I've rediscovered my passion for serving the customer. Here, look at some of the exercises in my journal."

As Martha thumbed through Paul's answers, she began to smile, and the smile grew broader with each line she read. "That's what we had hoped to accomplish, Paul. I can see now why Lew and Gary are so high on you, and why they wanted you to undergo these exercises to become a Serving Salesperson. I can see a passion and a fire in your eyes that wasn't there a month ago, and it excites me for Petra, it excites me for your customers, but most of all it excites me for you. You now see that when you blend the passion for serving your customers with the perseverance to see the sale through to its conclusion, you're well down the road to developing the grit necessary to meet your customers' needs, truly serve them, and work to transform your relationship with them," Martha said. "And when you do that consistently the sky truly is the limit. What I see in you now reminds me of a verse from the Bible, James 1:4: 'Let perseverance finish its work so that you may be mature and complete, not lacking anything.' You're ready to move on to talk to Lydia James about the third Pillar: Sharpen your EQ.

"Well done!"

Sharpen Your EQ

*When dealing with people, remember you are not dealing
with creatures of logic, but with creatures of emotion.*

– Dale Carnegie

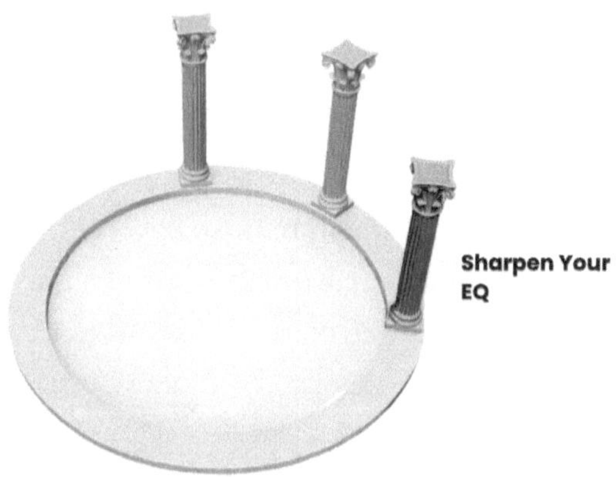

A New Year Brings a New Beginning

THE NEXT MEMBER of the TBS that Paul was to interview was Lydia
Thomas, a highly successful commercial real estate salesperson. Like
the other members of the TBS, her reputation certainly preceded her.
It seemed that just about every other one of the For Sale or Lease signs
in front of a commercial building had her name on it. Not only had she
sold or leased millions of dollars of commercial real estate, but she also
had won several awards and recognition from many civic organizations
for her support of their philanthropic initiatives.

As Paul pulled into her office parking lot the first Monday after
New Year's, he stopped to pause and reflect on the events of the last
couple of months. It struck him that like the beginning of a New Year,
he too was sensing a new beginning. The serving attitude that he was

adopting into his daily activities was beginning to result in deeper and more fruitful relationships with his customers and coworkers.

He was also improving as his relationship with his daughters and with Mary was beginning to thaw. Both he and his daughters now looked forward to their weekends together, and the last time he had dropped the girls off, Mary had invited him in for a cup of coffee. For the first time in a long time, they had a civil conversation. She had even invited him to go to one of Elizabeth's dance contests, which he eagerly accepted. Yes, it was more than just a New Year; it truly was a new beginning.

Paul found Lydia's office to be a hubbub of activity. She waved at him from behind her cluttered desk and then came around to greet him.

"Welcome, Paul, it's so nice to meet you!" she said, clasping his extended hand with hers in a warm handshake. Paul found Lydia to be a very professional and confident woman whom he guessed to be in her early fifties. Her enthusiasm was contagious and her presence truly lit up the room. Paul liked her instantly, and like the other members of the TBS she made him feel relaxed right away.

Lydia walked Paul into a conference room and offered him some coffee, which he gratefully accepted to help ward off the January chill. As they took seats across from each other at the conference table, Lydia began by asking questions first about himself and then about his first two interviews. After a few minutes Lydia asked him, "So, I'm here to talk about the third Pillar of being a Serving Salesperson: Sharpen Your EQ. Shall we get started?"

"The title for this Pillar intrigues me, Lydia," Paul began. "I'm familiar with the five competencies of emotional intelligence, and those really haven't really changed that much over the years. So I'm curious as to what is involved in learning how to sharpen your emotional intelligence, your EQ."

Lydia smiled the same knowing smile that Paul had seen with the other members of the TBS he had interviewed. She began with a question. "How have you seen the B2B buying process evolve in the last few years?"

Paul thought for a minute. "Well, there's really been quite a bit of change. The most obvious is how the pandemic increased the practice of virtual selling and digital marketing, which we find many of the younger customers prefer. We've had to implement an omnichannel marketing strategy to address the needs of individuals from different functional areas that are involved in the buying group. Finally, there are more people involved in the buying process, so it takes much longer."

"So then," Lydia continued, "how do you see these changes in the buying process impacting the emotional intelligence we need to exhibit to be successful?"

A look of realization came over Paul's face. "We need to have a good understanding of how the changes in our customers' buying process affect the way they approach their purchase journey. We then need to account for those changes in how we apply our own emotional intelligence."

"That's exactly it," said Lydia. "We need to factor in the impact of these changes and then decide how we need to modify our sales approach. You don't need to make wholesale changes in the five competencies of emotional intelligence," she continued. "You just need to sharpen your EQ to account for those changes. Once you have integrated the principles of the first two Pillars into your approach, having a sharpened EQ is the next step in transforming the relationship with your customer. John Philips will talk more about how your understanding of EQ will help you when you set about working to change your customers' perspective and then elevating their thinking from being mired in their problems to discovering new possibilities. You'll learn more about this when you speak with him.

"Now, we're going to discuss the five competencies of emotional intelligence and then weave in how changes in the buying environment need to be considered in our emotional intelligence practices. Okay?"

Making the Modifications

"We know that having a high EQ has a much greater impact—as much as a four-fold impact—on a person's success than having a high IQ does," continued Lydia. "Do you remember the five generally accepted competencies of emotional intelligence?"

"Sure: self-awareness, self-regulation, motivation, empathy, and social skills."

"And which one do you we usually start with, and can you give a short description of it?"

"Self-awareness," Paul answered, "is about recognizing and understanding your own emotions—what you're feeling and why. It's about knowing your strengths and weaknesses and understanding how your emotions affect those around you. It's also knowing what your personal and professional goals are and where you're headed in life and why. Basically, it's your value system and your moral compass."

"Very good, Paul," Lydia said with a smile. "Now, when you think about changes in the purchase process you mentioned, how do you need to factor those changes in to sharpen your self-awareness?"

The Five Competencies of Emotional Intelligence

Self-awareness

Self-regulation

Motivation

Empathy

Social skills

Paul thought for a minute. "As I think about what I've learned from my interviews and what I've read about," he said, "we need to be self-aware of our own personal preferences. Then we need to put those preferences aside and focus on how our customers are approaching their buying decision."

"A good start, Paul," said Lydia. "And we also need to understand that before making any contact with you, your customers will be anywhere from 40 to 70 percent through the purchase process and will have done a lot of research on your company before initiating that contact.

"We also know that we can no longer depend solely on communicating through personal interactions but need to have that omnichannel marketing strategy you mentioned. That strategy will allow your customers to gain whatever information they are seeking, through whatever medium they desire, at whatever point they are on their purchase journey. And all this needs to be done in a very user-friendly manner."

Lydia paused for a moment. "The research they've done on you," she continued, "will have made them knowledgeable about your company and your products, and they will expect you to be just as knowledgeable about their industry, their company, their products, and their competitors. It is becoming increasingly clear that B2B customers have the same expectations when making online purchases in a B2B setting as they do in a B2C setting and expect us to be able to answer complex questions quickly, concisely, and completely.

"We also need to think about the measures we might take to positively influence the way our customer perceives our product. Phoebe Andrews will talk more about this when she talks to you about communicating for impact, but a key factor in taking your customers' interests into account is to discover what their goals and objectives are for the situation they find themselves in. Phoebe will mention ways to elevate their perspective from where they are to where they could be.

Paul thought for a minute then said, "Wow! I need to make a more conscious effort to broaden my own self-awareness to account for the changes we have discussed."

"A good start. Now, what's the generally recognized second competency of emotional intelligence?" Lydia asked.

On to Self-Regulation

"Self-regulation," Paul answered. "What I remember about this is that once a self-aware person understands their emotions and the impact those emotions have on other people, the next step becomes managing those emotions. In addition to managing those emotions we must also manage any actions or reactions that the behavior of others might trigger in us. Self-regulation allows a person to stay true to their values and hold themselves personally accountable for whatever shortcomings might occur."

"So, how do the changes in the buying process you mentioned factor in your self-regulation during that process?" Lydia asked.

Paul thought for a moment. "Well, we need to adjust how we're going to approach the interactions with our customers. A study I read about found that the reason many customers prefer to do research online instead of interacting with a sales representative is because they feel the sales representative will promote their own agenda rather than seeking to solve the customer's problem. Customers want a salesperson who listens to their needs and then endeavors to provide them with the information they are looking for."

"So, what does this mean for you?" Lydia asked.

Paul thought for a minute. "For me," he said, "I need to sharpen my self-regulation by not only asking pertinent questions but also by focusing on listening effectively, listening with intent to understand rather than with the intent to respond. When my customer is talking, I often find myself thinking about what I'm going to say next. As a Serving Salesperson I cannot do that. Instead, I need to focus on *understanding* the issue the customer is facing, not simply *diagnosing* it.

---

*A Serving Salesperson needs to focus on understanding
the issue the customer is facing, not simply diagnosing it*

"Hold that thought on effective listening," said Lydia. "We're going to talk about another reason for listening effectively in just a bit. In the meantime, let's discuss motivation."

Motivation

Paul hesitated for a minute before speaking.

"Before I began these interviews, if I was really being honest, my main motivation for making a sale was what I could get out of it for myself—the money, the recognition, the rewards, things like that. I must confess that for the last few years doing things for me was what got me going and kept me going. However, I've come to realize that the total focus on what *I* could get out of sales was really leading me down the wrong path."

Lydia once again smiled that knowing smile. "So, how have your motivations changed?"

"Matthew emphasized that as a Serving Salesperson you no longer make sales calls. Instead, your purpose is to make serving calls. That's how I'm focusing my efforts now. When you focus on serving your customer and setting that as your true north, you really do look at the world differently. Now, when I'm dealing with customers, my motivation is to dig beneath the surface and attempt to truly *understand* their needs. Once I understand those needs, I'm beginning to think about how I can positively transform my relationship with them. I then focus on trying to work together with them to find a solution that works for both parties."

Lydia smiled again. "That's very insightful, Paul. I can see that these interviews are guiding you on the path to becoming a Serving Salesperson. Shall we talk about empathy?"

Paul's expression changed to show a bit of stress. "Do we have to?" he said.

Empathy

"Well, I wasn't expecting that for an answer," said Lydia, "can you elaborate a bit more on why the resistance?"

"It's just that I've never been good at being empathic," Paul replied. "Oh, we talk a lot about it in our meetings at work and I can cite chapter and verse on what it means to be empathetic. Seeing things from another person's perspective. Feeling their emotions. Moving around to the customer's side of the table to gain a better understanding of their situation. I know that putting yourself in your customers' shoes can help lead you to act with compassion and to do what you can to improve their situation. I also know that if a salesperson can do that, they can reduce the customer's stress as well as their own."

"So why is that so difficult for you?" asked Lydia.

"It's just not the way I'm wired," said Paul. "I have really tried to work with my customers to be empathic, but it doesn't seem to take long before I suddenly find myself driving them toward the solution that I think is right for them."

"So, how's that working for you?" asked Lydia.

Paul looked up and through gritted teeth said, "Not very well. When I first started out in sales I was dealing mainly with engineering and analytical types who looked at the world pretty much the same way I did. I would go in, show them the specifications, talk about facts and figures, answer their questions, and usually make the sale. Now the buying groups are much larger, come from all different departments with different priorities, and usually have a greater percentage of younger people in them. It just seems that I'm not as successful as I used to be."

"I can relate, Paul," Lydia began, settling back in her chair. "I pretty much operated the same way when I started out. I'm analytical, and, like you, I wanted to get straight to the point, to what I saw being the issue at hand, to focusing on the numbers and the spreadsheets. I thought that all my customers looked at a lease or purchase the same way I did—basically the facts and figures on the agreement and what the financials would be. However, early on I was not having very much success and was seriously considering getting out of the business."

"So what happened?" Paul asked.

"Well, one day at a networking event, one of the senior partners came up to me with another gentlemen and said, 'Lydia, I'd like you to meet Darrin Lee. I thought you might enjoy talking with him.'

"Well, everyone in our business knew Darrin Lee. He was generally recognized as the dean of the local commercial real estate agents. I knew him to be very knowledgeable and had heard he was willing to share his knowledge and especially enjoyed mentoring those new to the business."

Now she had Paul's attention. "So what happened?" he asked.

A Key Word

"Darrin couldn't have been more gracious. It was clear from the very beginning of our conversation that he was one of those rare salespeople who had an abundance mentality—there's enough business out there for everyone, so let's help each other out. He began by asking me a few questions: Why was I in commercial real estate? How did I approach my customers? How did I find out their needs? And so forth. He then asked me if I had any questions for him. I mustered up the courage to ask him how he was so successful, how he went about finding out his customers' needs, and how he was able to parlay that into showing empathy to his clients. He smiled and said, 'It all comes down to one word.'

Paul leaned forward in his chair. "One word? What was it?" he asked.

Lydia paused a moment for effect.

"*Curiosity.*"

"Curiosity? Why curiosity?"

"Think for a minute, Paul. If you're curious about something or someone, what does that show about you?"

"It shows that you're interested, that you want to know more, that you want to explore the situation in more detail to gain a better understanding of what that person is going through."

"You want to know what else Darrin told me?"

"Yes, please."

> *If you're curious about something or someone it shows that you're interested, that you want to know more.*

"He said, 'Infuse curiosity with empathy,'" Lydia continued. "Aren't all successful salespeople curious—curious about what issues their customers are facing, curious about what an optimal solution would look like for their customers? Don't we ask a lot of questions about all those things?"

Paul nodded.

"So," Lydia continued, "let's talk about one more key element to the process. We call it Peeling the Onion. Have you ever peeled an onion?"

"A few times."

"When you peel the skin off, what's underneath it?"

"The first layer."

"And if you peel off the first layer, what's underneath that?"

"The second layer."

"And if you peel that?"

"The third layer," said Paul, wanting this to end.

Lydia continued. "In sales, the first layer is the first question you ask your customer. Now here's the key point. The customer's real problems are not at the first layer. They're down at the second and third layers. However, most salespeople want to jump right in and solve the first-layer problem. What we need to do is use the answers from the first layer and peel the onion to get down to the second and third layers.

"Here's where we show we're a true Serving Salesperson. It's at the second and third layers where we infuse curiosity with empathy. When asking follow-up questions, we want to show empathy by asking questions that allow you to discover the future implications of the problem they mentioned. Use words like *implication, effect, consequences, impact, ramifications,* and *repercussions.*"

Lydia could see a bit of confusion on Paul's face, so she continued, "Asking questions about what implications this issue has for the customer shows that not only are you *curious* about the issues they are having but will also show *empathy* by trying to understand their situation. This also helps you identify the emotions that go along with that. You'll hear about their concerns, frustrations, anxieties, anger—all which give you a better picture of what they're dealing with. You can then respond accordingly.

"Tell you what," Lydia said, "let me give you a scenario. Assume that you're in one of your customers' factories where a machine has broken down. What types of questions would you ask about the implications of that breakdown not only to be curious but also to show empathy, to see things from their perspective, and to understand the implications of that machine breaking down?"

"Well, I guess I'd ask about the impact of not getting their product on time would have on their customer's business operation," Paul said. "Also, I'd ask what problems any delays might affect the customer's ability to serve their customers and how not getting their orders out on time might lead their customer to switch to another supplier."

"See what you just did?" Lydia said. "You were *curious* by peeling the onion down to the second and third layer but also showed *empathy* by inquiring about the impact the delay had on their operation. While being curious is important, infusing that curiosity with empathy really helps to put yourself in their shoes.

"If you remember, Pillar Seven is titled Guide the Transformation. A key element in beginning the transformation process is *discovery*—helping your customers to discover a solution that initiates the transformation that you can lead them in. Transforming the relationship with your customer involves using your sharpened EQ to formulate a questioning strategy that guides your customer toward elevating their perspective around what they aspire to be their optimal solution. As you're peeling the onion, you can ask the customer solution-centered questions that would begin to explore what their aspirations are—what they would perceive an ideal outcome to be. Phoebe Andrews will talk more about this, and John Philips will go into more detail when you meet with him later on, but you can get a start on the transformation process here by beginning to explore the outcome they aspire to."

Perceived Risk

"Having empathy also means that you understand the *perceived risk* that buyers face during the purchase journey. Buyers often make weighty financial decisions that could have a significant impact on their organization, their colleagues, and even themselves. Unlike consumers making purchase decisions for themselves, buyers must balance their personal risk tolerance—and sometimes their career prospects—along with the interests of their employer. They know that making a wrong decision could have significant financial consequences on the organizations as well as on them personally.

"Therefore, perceived risk looms large in the minds of B2B customers and can have an important impact on their actions as they proceed through their purchase journey. Research has found that a consequence of the perceived risk buyers feel they are facing is that they frequently make *defensive decisions*. That means they are selecting what they perceive to be the safest choice rather than what may be the most optimal choice. The study found that over 40 percent of the buyers admitted they make defensive purchase decisions more than 70 percent of the time. The study also found that less than a third of the buyers considered themselves to be risk tolerant."

"Very interesting," responded Paul. "I've been noticing more of what I'd call a defensive posture with some of the buyer groups I've been dealing with, especially the larger ones. I can now see why building trust is even more important."

"Building trust is really the remedy to risk and is a key factor in transforming your relationship with the customer," answered Lydia. "Trust really serves to bridge the gap between a buyer's risk-averse tendencies and the risk you present as a vendor wanting them to change. You'll learn more about building trust when you talk with Marcos Simón next month.

Effective Listening

"Let's get back to the topic of effective listening. It's important to be an effective listener, right?"

Paul gave a sheepish grin and said, "With my straight-ahead style I'm afraid I'm often guilty of letting my mind race ahead to thinking how I'm going to respond rather than trying to focus on what the customer is saying. I need to resist the urge to jump in and instead concentrate on listening to everything the customer is saying and then clarifying the key issues. I then need to ask more follow-up questions to make sure I understand what their needs are. I know we're supposed to listen with the intent to understand rather than with the intent to respond, but that's really hard for me," he said with a tone of resignation in his voice.

Lydia replied, "It's hard for everybody and is a paradigm shift for most salespeople. However, if you focus on listening with the intent to understand rather than with the intent to respond, you can often uncover a crucial issue the customer is having.

"As we're being curious and listening effectively," Lydia continued, "we must also listen for the unmet need—a need the customer mentions, often casually, that if you explore further can go from an offhand remark to a critical issue that the customer might not even realize they have."

By listening with the intent to understand rather than with the intent to respond, you can often uncover a crucial issue the customer is having.

"So how do we do that?" Again, he recognized the knowing TBS smile.

"Here's one more thing we've learned when peeling the onion with our customers that can allow you to dig deeper, to sometimes find the unmet need," Lydia said.

"What's that?" Paul asked, now leaning forward.

"It's the *power of silence*," Lydia said. "What we've learned is that after you've peeled the onion down to the second or third layers and the customer has given you their answer, remain silent, even though your natural tendency is to respond immediately. We teach our people to be silent for at least five seconds in these types of situations. The customer will often continue to expand on the problem they have or may even talk about a new problem—their unmet need. We can then be more curious, ask more questions, and keep peeling the onion. The more curious we are and the more empathy we show, the more likely we are to discover an unmet need.

"Finally," Lydia said, "respecting diversity and inclusion is a vital aspect of empathy, as is communication. You need to pay close attention to what you and others say whether verbally or through body language."

"Wow," Paul said quietly, "you've given me a lot to think about and even more to work on. I am really beginning to see how the Pillars of being a Servings Salesperson fit together. Thank you so much for sharing this information with me."

"You're more than welcome, Paul. I'm glad you found this discussion useful and that you're seeing how the Pillars of being a Serving Salesperson build on one another. Why don't we take a quick break before we discuss social skills?"

Social Skills

After refreshing their coffees Lydia continued, "Other than the obvious business etiquette that our jobs require us to have when we interact with others, how do we need to sharpen our EQ around social skills?"

"I guess I'll build on the empathy dimension—developing an understanding of others' feelings and attempting to understand their perspective," Paul answered.

Lydia smiled. "That's not quite it. Let's go back to our earlier discussion of the change in the composition of the buying groups. How might sharpening your social skills be of benefit there?"

Paul thought for a minute. "Well," he said, "the buying groups are getting larger and the purchase process is taking longer. With more people involved in the buying group we are going to have to deal with different social styles and different sets of purchase criteria. I think that would take more social skills."

"You're on the right track," said Lydia, leaning forward in her chair. "You've mentioned the buying side. What changes are you noticing on the selling side?"

Paul thought for a minute and then the light bulb came on. "Wow! There are also more people involved in the sales process, and I'm involved in a lot of selling being done in teams with subject matter experts involved. So, we also need to understand how to interact with people on the selling side of the equation as well as those on the buying side. I've sometimes had customers ask to talk with either my manager, the engineers who worked on the product design, and even the supply chain people, so I need to know how to bring them into the conversation."

"You've just hit on a key point of understanding the social skills dimension, Paul. Think about it. When making important business decisions, nothing of consequence gets accomplished alone. You're always going to be working with others to bring whatever situation you're dealing with to a successful conclusion. You're also going to have to understand, work with, and collaborate with others on the selling side to reach that decision." Lydia could see Paul bristle at what she had just said. "Tell me why you reacted just the way you did?"

When making important business decisions, nothing of consequence gets accomplished alone.

"I've seen this coming, and it's not what I wanted to hear, but I know I'm going to have to accept it. I've always taken a lone wolf approach in my sales strategy, always wanting to do things on my own. However, in light of some recent events, I've come to realize that my lone wolf philosophy has sometimes been a detriment to me and to our company."

"So what do you intend to do about it?"

"I need to spend more time developing relationships with my coworkers who have the skills and expertise that I can draw upon to solve a customer's problem. I also need to nurture those relationships with subject matter experts inside and even outside the company who I might call upon to solve a customer's issue."

Paul hesitated for a minute.

"Here's what I'm taking away from this part of our discussion," he said. "While I know it's important to be able to build rapport with your customers, I'm discovering it's equally important to build rapport and develop meaningful connections with those inside and sometimes outside your company as well. As you said, nothing of consequence gets done alone, and now I have a better handle on how to involve others in the sales effort as needed."

Lydia settled back in her chair and looked Paul straight in the eye.

Summarizing 'Sharpen Your EQ'

"So, what do you think about sharpening your EQ, now Paul?"

Paul smiled a rather sheepish smile. "I have to tell you," he said, "that I really wondered why this Pillar was included in being a Serving Salesperson," replied Paul. "I thought EQ is EQ, I'm pretty good at it, so why do we need to discuss it? Spending time with you, Lydia, has really opened my eyes to how the ongoing changes in the sales environment call for us to continue to sharpen our EQ. Thank you very much for your insight."

"Oh, no thanks necessary," said Lydia with a casual wave of her hand. "You didn't think you were done with me, did you?"

Paul knew what was coming. "No, I fully expected you to give me an assignment," he said with a grin.

"There are several assessments you can do online to measure your emotional intelligence, which you'll find in your notebook," Lydia said. "Petra will cover the cost of two of these assessments. By completing these, you'll get a better sense of the EQ elements you might need to work on. I'm also going to supply you with some materials on how to deal with this new, younger generation of B2B customers."

Lydia stood up indicating the meeting was over. "I think you'll find many of these readings very eye-opening and you'll begin to get a sense of things you can do to sharpen your EQ," she said. With a final firm handshake, she escorted Paul out.

It wasn't long before Paul had a chance to put his newly sharpened EQ into practice.

An EQ Test

About a week after his meeting with Lydia, Paul was on what he thought would be a routine sales call to a customer that had just been assigned to him. Ron Taylor at the Paragon Company had called and told Paul they were having some issues with one of the sensors that controlled the HVAC process in one part of their production plant. This was the first opportunity Paul had had to meet Ron face-to-face.

Ron took Paul to the part of the plant where the sensor was located, pointed out the affected sensor, and said, "This one has been causing us a lot of problems lately. Let's get a replacement ordered and get things back to normal again."

Before his time with Lydia, Paul would have taken down the necessary information, got the new sensor ordered and installed, and moved on. However, Paul thought first about peeling the onion and next about infusing empathy with curiosity and listening for the unmet need. He began to ask Ron a few more questions. "Tell me how the other sensors are working for you," he said.

"We've had another one go off and on a couple of times, but it seems to be working okay now."

Paul resisted the urge to respond. He said simply, "Hmm" and then remained silent. After a few seconds Ron spoke up.

"Now that we're talking about it, some of the guys in that part of the plant mention that the temperature can get uncomfortable pretty quickly."

Paul's ears perked up. It sounded like something was off. He had heard the HVAC system was a bit dated, but having issues with two of the sensors was unusual. Paul asked to be taken to the locations of the other sensors and talked to a couple of other workers in those sections. He learned that there had been several short interruptions of the HVAC system in other parts of the plant that Ron was not aware of.

Paul asked Ron to take him back to the main HVAC unit where Paul took off the panel to the main wiring. While he wasn't an engineer, what he saw didn't look right to him. Some of the wiring looked a bit frayed and discolored, which set off alarm bells in Paul's head. Shining the light from his phone around the wiring box, he saw the sticker that had the maintenance history. The last time the system was serviced was three years ago.

"Is this date right?" he asked Ron.

"I guess so," said Ron. "I must confess we have not been as diligent with our maintenance as we should have been."

"I'm not an engineer, but something doesn't look quite right to me here. Let me take a picture of this and send it to one of our maintenance engineers to get his opinion."

Paul sent the picture to Joe Ladd, one of Petra's engineers. He gave it a minute to make sure the picture had time to get there and then called Joe.

"Hi, Joe. Did you see the picture of this HVAC unit out here at Paragon I just sent you?"

"Let me look. Wow! Tell me more."

As Paul described what he saw he could hear the concern in Joe's voice.

"I'll be right there," Joe said.

Less than an hour later Paul, Ron, and Joe were looking at Paragon's main HVAC unit. Joe took off some more panels and shined his flashlight into the interior of the unit, and shined his flashlight into the interior of the unit and let out a concerned, "Oh." He then went to check some other things. He was back after a few minutes. "This unit is twenty-two years old. The normal life expectancy is twelve to fifteen years. It's living on borrowed time. We need to replace this unit immediately."

A look of obvious concern came over Ron's face. "I don't know if we have money in the budget for this. Can't we let it go for a while?"

Joe looked straight at Ron and replied, "I strongly recommend you replace this entire unit immediately. With the present condition of this wiring, if you continue to operate this unit, there is a very strong possibility of it shorting out. That could cause a fire. With the flammable materials you have in this plant, the result could be disastrous. Ron, it's a good thing you brought Paul back here when you did. A fire could have started here just about any time."

Ron took off his hard hat and ran his fingers through his hair. "Well," he said, "we've trusted Petra with handling our system for as long as I've been here. When can we get the unit replaced?"

Joe made a quick call to the warehouse. "We can get the main unit delivered on special-order tomorrow morning. We have the rest of what you would need in stock, and I can have a team out here to-morrow. As it's late in the afternoon on Thursday, I'd shut everything down now and give your workers a day off tomorrow. We'll start as soon as the unit gets here and should be able to get it installed by late afternoon or evening. Once we get everything up and running, we'll check all the sensors around the plant and make sure everything's in good working order. We should have you ready to be back up and running by Monday morning."

Joe left and Paul could tell that Ron was overwhelmed by what had just happened and knew showing some empathy was in order. "Let's go get a cup of coffee," Paul suggested, "and I can tell you how this process is going to work."

"Good idea," Ron replied. "My head is really spinning right now."

The Aftermath

Paul spent the next half-hour sitting across from Ron with a cup of coffee in the company's lunch area, assuaging his concerns.

"I just can't believe it was that serious," Ron kept saying while shaking his head. "We really could have had a disaster on our hands."

"But now you're not going to," said Paul, reaching over and gently grasping Ron's forearm. "Joe and his team have done this same process any number of times. They know what they're doing, and they'll have you back up and running tomorrow and you can be fully operational by Monday."

As the conversation began to wane, Paul could sense that Ron's emotions had leveled out to the point where he could leave. "Well, unless you have any more questions for me, I'll be going," said Paul. "I'll come out here with Joe and his team tomorrow to make sure the process gets started okay and to make sure they have everything they need. I'm positive they will as they're very experienced, but I'll be here just in case."

Ron looked up with a dazed look still on his face. "That would be nice, Paul," he said, rising part way out of this chair and offering his hand. "Thanks for all your help," he said, plopping back down. Ron asked a worker who was right there to escort Paul out.

Paul was still in the parking lot on his phone when he saw Ron come running up to his car. He quickly got out of his car to meet Ron.

"Is everything okay?" Paul asked with a concerned voice.

"It is now," said Ron, a bit winded by his short jog to Paul's car. "I'm sorry that I got so emotional in there," he said, managing a smile. "It's just that in a very few minutes we went from what I thought was going to be a simple repair to understanding the seriousness of our situation to having to undertake a major project. I just got overwhelmed by it. After you left it hit me as to what an incredible service you and Joe just did and will be doing for us. Just by listening to me you uncovered a major problem that could have turned into a disaster. Again, I'm sorry I got so squirrely in there for a while, but I can't thank you enough first for finding what was a major problem, and second," he said with sheepish smile, "for taking the time to talk me off the ledge."

"It's our pleasure to serve you," said Paul offering his hand. "Serving our customers' needs is what we're all about at Petra."

A Realization

Paul spent the next couple of weeks immersed in readings about emotional intelligence and how the younger generation of B2B customers approaches their buying journey. He found all of what he read fascinating, so much so that he often couldn't put it down. He also found that his increased understanding of his and his customers' emotional intelligence was allowing him to understand his customers' and coworkers' motivations and needs in more depth and detail than he ever had before. He found himself having much more meaningful conversations with his customers about their problems and seeking the best way to solve those problems.

His weekends with the girls were different too. He used to dread them, but now he actually looked forward to them. He also spent a bit more time with Mary during pick-ups and drop-offs, much more than a few months earlier. Sometimes his girls would help him with his Serving Salesperson exercises, and he would call them more regularly on the new cell phones he had bought them for Christmas. On Sundays he used to drop the girls off at church and get on his computer at a local coffee shop. Now he would go into the service and usually find someone he had met during one of his men's ministry projects to sit with. While he would usually see Mary, he thought it was best for her to invite him to sit with her. So far, she hadn't.

One Sunday's sermon had a particular impact on him. The minister's message was entitled "Looking at the World Through Different Eyes" and was based on the Bible passage in Acts 9 where Saul, a Jewish rabbi whose life's mission to that point had been to persecute Christians, is blinded on the road to Damascus. He hears a voice saying "Saul, Saul, why do you persecute me?" He is led into Damascus, regains his sight, and eventually comes to be known by the Roman name of Paul, perhaps the greatest Christian apostle the world has ever known. The similarities between the changes that occurred to Saul on the road to Damascus and the changes that Paul was undergoing on his own road toward becoming a Serving Salesperson were not lost on him.

Paul was back at Lydia's office at the end of the month, watching her nod approvingly at the exercises that he had completed. "So, Paul, what do you think about the Sharpen your EQ Pillar now?"

"I must admit I was a little skeptical when we first began talking about this as I didn't feel my EQ needed any sharpening. However, the more I learned the more convinced I became that those with a better understanding of their own EQ as well as their customers' EQ have certainly shown to be more successful in their dealings with people, especially us salespeople."

"And how has that changed the way you deal with your customers?"

"In a dramatic fashion. I first work on setting my true north around serving my customers, blending the passion and perseverance to do so, and now sharpening my EQ to be able to understand my own and my customers' motivations better. I'm now finding that I'm able to put myself in their shoes, understand their challenges better, and am working to really transform my with relationship with them. So, yes, this has been a truly valuable exercise."

Lydia smiled broadly. "As Lew said, becoming a Serving Salesperson is a journey not a destination. I can see from what you've just said, the exercises you've completed, and your actions that your EQ is much higher than when you came here a few weeks ago. You need to continue sharpening your EQ as customers and their needs are constantly changing. As Philippians 2:3-4 says, 'Do nothing out of selfish ambition or vain conceit. Rather, in humility value others above yourselves, not looking to your own interests but each of you to the interests of the others.'

"It looks like my work here is done and I'm ready to pass you on to Marcos Simón, the next member of the TBS who will talk to you about the next Pillar: Build Trust Through the Human Touch.

"Well done!"

Build Trust Through the Human Touch

> *Pretend that every single person you meet has a sign around his or her neck that says, 'Make me feel important.' Not only will you succeed in sales, you will succeed in life.*
>
> – *Mary Kay Ash*

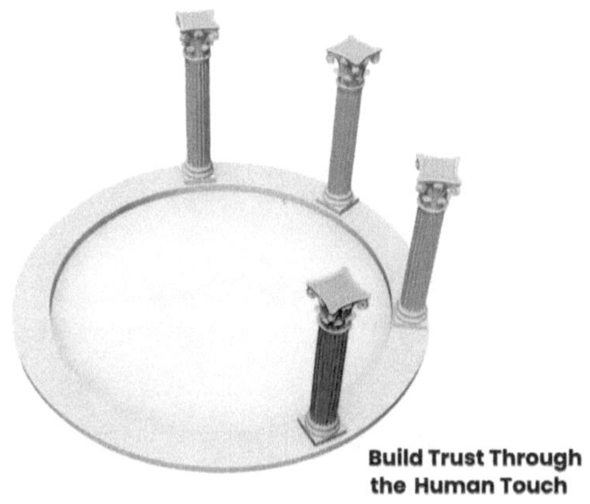

Build Trust Through the Human Touch

The Importance of Trust

IT WAS THE first week in February and Paul was sitting in an office at the Bickerton Industrial Supply Company across from Marcos Simón, who at first glance could have been mistaken for the company custodian. Casually dressed in blue jeans and a dark blue sweatshirt with the name of one of his product lines emblazoned in white across his chest, Marcos was a short, stocky, balding man in his late thirties. He was the youngest of any of the people he had interviewed so far. Marcos worked as the sales manager for Bickerton, a distributor of industrial products much like those Paul sold. Paul had spent many hours in businesses just like this with all the noise, activity, clutter, and chaos that accompanies such an environment. A few months ago, Paul would have dismissed anything Marcos said based on his appearance alone. However, the past few months had really opened his eyes to the fact that a Serving Salesperson can come from any walk of life, have any educational or cultural background, and can sell any type of product or service. Marcos leaned over his cluttered desk, gave Paul a firm handshake, and began to speak loud enough to be heard over the din of the background noise of the operation.

"So, tell me, what have you learned about being a Serving Salesperson so far?"

Paul summarized his first three interviews and finished with, "And that brings me to you, Marcos."

"I'm delighted to have the privilege to talk about this Pillar: Build Trust Through the Human Touch," said Marcos. After a brief hesitation he looked directly at Paul and continued, "Paul, would you say your customers trust you?"

Taken aback by Marcos's directness, Paul began to hesitate. "I don't know. . . I guess . . . I'd like to think so," he stammered.

"I asked you that question to get our conversation started," Marcos said with a smile. "Your answer is typical of most salespeople. Research shows that over 90 percent of B2B salespeople feel they are more honest than average and that their customers trusted their communications more than average. However, the sad truth is that the actual levels of trust are much, much lower—usually in the 50 to 60 percent range and have been in a steady decline for a long time."

Marcos continued, "We learned from a report on trust conducted by a large consulting firm that the most important factor in determining if a B2B company will decide to do business with you is simply *Do they trust you?* This is important because if a company trusts you, they are almost twice as likely to do business with you, twice as likely to recommend you, and are more willing to pay a premium price for your products. Also, after you've grounded yourself in the first three Pillars of being a Serving Salesperson, building trust with your customer is the next and very important step in to transforming your relationship with them. Building that trust is a key factor in the customer allowing you to let them guide you through their own transformation process that John Philips will talk about."

The most important factor in determining if a B2B company will decide to do business with you is simply Do they trust you?

"Wow!" said Paul. "I knew it was important to build trust with your clients, but I had no idea it was *that* important."

"And that's not all," Marcos continued. "I saw a survey that found that 97 percent of salespeople habitually and knowingly misrepresent their products and services. They confess they do it because 'everybody does it' and believe they'll never get caught doing it."

Paul silently thought of his own misguided efforts at deception. He was impressed with Marcos's sales knowledge and passion for selling with each passing minute. Marcos's insight into the sales process certainly belied his age and outward appearance.

"Why don't we get to the reason you're here," Marcos continued enthusiastically, "to learn about the fourth Pillar: Build Trust Through the Human Touch. Shall we begin?"

Defining Trust

Marcos leaned back in his chair and paused for a minute.

"So, Paul, would you please define *trust* for me?"

Thinking for a minute, Paul answered. "I'd say that trust is doing what you say you're going to do, when you said you're going to do it, and doing it consistently over time."

"A good start," said Marcos. "But is that enough? Is just doing what you said you're going to do *really* going to determine if your customers can trust you?"

Paul was drawing a blank. "I'm struggling here. I guess I don't have a good answer."

"We all struggle for a good answer," said Marcos. "That's because trust is an abstract, complicated, and multi-faceted concept that all B2B marketers aspire to achieve. And, like you, they all struggle to define it.

"When I began my sales career, I focused on what you said trust is—doing what I said I was going to do when I said I was going to do it. When I became the sales manager here, I realized there was more that my sales team and I could learn about building trust. I knew we needed to have a more concrete understanding of the actions and activities we could engage in that would allow our customers to trust us more. So, we began to dig around to see what information we could find about how to build trust in B2B sales."

Marcos stopped for a moment to take a drink from his coffee cup. "The sales process really comes down to the buyer having a set of expectations about the vendor's company, product, and salesperson," he continued. "As the buying journey progresses, the buyer will determine if those expectations are met based on the experiences the vendor company creates throughout that journey. There are two key points here. The first is that trust is developed when a vendor creates experiences that meet and sometimes exceed expectations. The second is that these experiences are created largely through interactions between people who are either direct representatives or advocates of the vendor organizations. Setting clear and concise expectations are important when you set about determining how the transformation you're trying to implement will transpire. If we do this right, it then leads to—"

"Building trust through the human touch," Paul said, finishing Marcos's sentence.

Trust is developed when a vendor creates experiences that meet and sometimes exceed expectations.

The Seven Levers of Trust

Marcos smiled and leaned forward and continued. "The primary result of the research I mentioned was that the consulting firm formulated what they designated as the Seven Levers of Trust that B2B companies should endeavor to create and fulfill in the trust-building process with their customers. Here, let me show them to you, and then let's discuss how these levers fit into the mindset of being a Serving Salesperson."

Marcos reached into a pile of papers on his desk and handed Paul a diagram with the seven levers listed.

The Seven Levers of Trust

Accountability

Consistency

Competence

Dependability

Empathy

Integrity

Transparency

"Wow! These are all traits that have come up in one form or another in my discussions with others about being a Serving Salesperson," Paul said. "So, practicing these behaviors would come naturally to a Serving Salesperson."

"Imagine that," Marcos said with a wink. "Now, three of these levers emerged as the ones that B2B customers considered the most important in the purchase process. Which of the levers do you think were most important?"

Paul looked at the list and thought for a moment.

"Well, competence and dependability for sure," Paul said. "B2B buyers would insist on those. Now for the third one, I know my customers look for consistency in what I provide them, so I'm going with consistency."

"That's right, Paul. You chose the same ones the study respondents did. One thing though, we're not saying the other levers are not important. However, what the report does say is that the three you mentioned were chosen as the most important to B2B buyers during their purchase journey.

"So, let's talk about what we as Serving Salespeople can to do exhibit competence, consistency, and dependability. Let's start with competence. How would you define *competence* and what can we as salespeople do to exhibit competence to our customers?"

Showing Competence

"Well," Paul began, "when I think of competence, I think of an individual who is recognized for their expertise that allows them to complete tasks successfully and efficiently."

"So how do we show that competence to our customers?"

Paul thought for a minute and then said, "The first thing that comes to mind is that we need to show that we're the expert—an expert on our products and how they can be used to resolve any issues the customer might have."

"Let's keep going," said Marcos. "What else do we need to do to show we're an expert? What did Lydia James say a potential customer is going to do before they contact you?"

"Do research on us, check out our website, look at any customer reviews, things like that."

"So, what does this tell you about something you need to do?"

Paul opened his eyes wide and exclaimed, "We need to do research on our customers like they've done on us."

"That's right," said Marcos. "Remember that you need to come across as the expert. That means you need to do research to find out as much as you can about their industry; their company; their products; their competition; and any technical, legal, or environmental issues they might be facing. They're going to know a lot about you. You need to know just as much or maybe even more about them. Not only do they *want* you to know that information, but they also *expect* you to know that information. Also, if you're going to transform your relationship with them by building trust, you need to have a good understanding of their company and their industry. Being an expert and exhibiting competence go hand in hand," Marcos said. "When you think of someone who's an expert, what do you think of? How can someone show they have the competence that makes people think of them as an expert? What have they done? What have they accomplished?"

Paul' thought for a minute. "I look at things like their years of experience, their educational background, any specialized training they have received, or any certifications they may have earned," he said. "I also look as to whether they are involved in any professional associations." Paul hesitated for a moment and then continued. "I also think of someone who is identified as being a thought leader—someone who has provided valuable insights to the industry through things like online posts, blogs, and maybe publishing articles in trade magazines or even an academic journal."

"Good points, Paul," responded Marcos. "So whatever measures you can take to gain some additional training or certification will add to your credibility. Also think about what and where you can post or publish to be considered a thought leader. Some folks here have written and posted how-to guides on using some of our products, and a couple have even recorded instructional videos."

Showing Consistency

"Now, Paul, let's talk about consistency. Define *consistency* for me and then give me your thoughts on how a salesperson can show consistency."

Paul leaned back in his chair and thought for a minute. "When you're consistent," he began, "you've established a reputation of behaving or performing in a similar way over time. When you're known as being consistent, people can rely on your behavior or performance and plan accordingly."

"The 'over time' piece is important," said Marcos. "Buyers look very favorably upon companies, products, and individuals that show consistency in product and financial performance over an extended period over time. So, Paul, what have you done at Petra to show your consistency?"

"At Petra we discussed how our customers expect and even demand being able to access information through multiple channels, so we designed an omnichannel marketing strategy. We know we have to be consistent in our messaging across our marketing channels. We can't be saying one thing through one channel and a different thing through another channel. We know we simply can't risk confusing the customers."

"Good thoughts," said Marcos with a smile. "Now, let's talk about dependability. How about giving me a definition, and then tell me how we can show that we're dependable?"

Showing Dependability

"This goes back to the 'setting expectations' aspect you mentioned earlier," Paul said. "If people see you as dependable, you've developed the expectation that you will be available and reliable. You also have shown your customers that you understand them and their needs almost to the point where you can predict and meet those needs," Paul answered.

"Good again," said Marcos. "Now remember we began our conversation talking about buyers entering an interaction with their salespeople with a set of expectations. How does being dependable enter in setting expectations?"

"I've run into this too many times," said Paul with a sigh. "I learned the hard way. To the best of my ability, I need to educate my customers on what, when, and how things are going to happen. To be dependable we first need to be clear and concise in setting our customers' expectations." Paul paused to take a drink and then continued, "I then make meeting those expectations my priority. Based on my conversation with you and others, I know I need to respond to customer inquiries promptly, accurately, and concisely. I've also learned that I need to be proactive and provide concise and regular communication about the progress of the sale delivered in the form and media most favored by my customers. This is especially important when the news is not positive. While customers don't like to be told things they don't want to hear, it's much better to be up front and honest with them."

"And one more thing," said Marcos. "Remember when Martha Peters talked about having grit? That enters in here as well. We need to make sure that we exhibit the perseverance to follow through to the end of the customer's buying journey. Our customers need to be able to depend on us to not only be there at the end of the journey but to be available to answer any post-purchase questions even after the product or service is delivered. We know that sometimes customers have buyer's remorse and feel that they've made the wrong purchase. Being dependable also means being there to assure them that they've made the right decision and sometimes even hold their hand.

Now," Marcos continued, "we've covered a fair amount of ground so far and my coffee cup is empty. How about we take a break and get some more coffee and give you a chance to digest what we've talked about so far?" Marcos said, getting up out of his chair and leading Paul out the door.

Marcos and Paul were a few steps down the hall when an administrative assistant came up to them. "Marcos, I'm sorry to interrupt, but Andy from Forum is on the phone, and he says it's important that he talk to you."

"Been working on that order for about six weeks," said Marcos with a wink. "Would you excuse me for a minute, Paul?"

"Of course, I totally understand," said Paul, stepping out of the way so Marcos could return to his office.

While waiting for Marcos to finish his phone call, Paul struck up a conversation with the salesperson in the office next to Marcos's. She was a pleasant young woman named Olivia who looked to be in her late twenties. "I understand that you're in here talking to Marcos about one of the Pillars of being a Serving Salesperson," said Olivia. "I assume it's Build Trust Through the Human Touch?"

Paul nodded.

"Marcos is really a good person to talk about that, especially after all he's been through," she said.

"I guess I'm not sure what you're talking about," responded Paul with mild surprise.

"Oh really? I'm surprised it hasn't come up as Marcos is truly a living example of building trust with his customers. A little over four years ago, Marcos was diagnosed with cancer. He had a tough go of it for a while. He had to go through some debilitating treatments which forced him to miss a lot of work for most of a year. While our health insurance covered most of his medical bills, being a straight commission salesperson Marcos was worried about the lost income and how he would be able to provide for his family."

"So how was he able to make it through?" asked Paul.

"That's really the cool part," said Olivia. "Unbeknownst to Marcos, when his biggest customer found out about his situation, he got a bunch of Marcos' other customers together on a video conference to see what they could do to help him. He then called one of our owners and told her how Marcos was one of the very few salespeople they could really trust. They said they wanted to do right by him and were all going to keep placing orders with Bickerton, but only if Marcos got the commissions.

"Wow!" said Paul, "so what happened?"

Olivia smiled and said, "Not only did he not lose any income, but his customers placed so many orders that we had to hire an inside salesperson to come in and take them. The revenue generated from these sales was enough not only to cover Marcos's lost income and benefits but paid for the person we hired as well. "And I can't begin to tell you the number of phone calls, emails, cards, letters, and prayers that Marcos received. He said all of that was a big factor in his recovery. He's been in remission for going on two years now, and he just received a clean bill of health at his last checkup. Yes, Marcos is truly a living example of how to build trust through the human touch."

Paul could hear Marcos approaching down the hallway. "Nice talking with you, Olivia," he said, taking a couple of steps into the hallway. He hesitated and leaned back into Olivia's office. "And thanks," he said softly.

"She didn't tell you any lies about me, did she?" Marcos asked with a smile as they continued their walk to the break room.

"No, quite the contrary," said Paul, now looking at Marcos with even more respect than just a few minutes before.

After returning to Marcos's office with full cups of coffee, they continued their conversation.

Adding the Human Touch

Marcos began, "Now, let's talk about how the human touch enters into—"

"Excuse me for interrupting you, Marcos, but I'm really confused about how to add the human touch nowadays," interjected Paul with a twinge of nervousness in his voice. "I've read and have experienced how B2B customers are moving away from personal interactions and more toward purchasing their products online. I've also seen some predictions that eventually the vast majority of B2B sales will be conducted digitally. How do we incorporate the human touch then?"

"I understand that concern," said Marcos, with an assuring nod. "However, let's talk about what the research says and how we as salespeople can still provide the human touch for our customers.

"We know that a lot of our B2B customers will continue to be digitally native millennials with the Gen Zs coming right behind them. These age groups are accustomed to the easier, faster, and more streamlined ways of purchasing products for themselves. They have come to expect the same experience in their B2B purchases. Despite what some of the research says, and as Lydia James alluded to, however, customers will still want to be able to interact with a sales representative that they perceive is looking out for their best interests. That leads right into the advantage we as Serving Salespeople can offer. Also, if the customer does feel we're looking out for their best interests, they are more likely to trust us to guide them through their own transformation process."

"But how do we provide the human touch to those customer groups who say they prefer little or no personal contact with a salesperson?"

Customers will still want to be able to interact with a sales representative that they perceive is looking out for their best interests

---

"A word we're beginning to hear more in B2B marketing is *hyper-personalization*," Marcos continued. "Hyper-personalization refers to combining the personal information we know about customer behaviors with such elements as real-time data, artificial intelligence, and machine learning to provide data-driven insights that create a tailored and relevant experience. Technology will no doubt continue to improve and there's no question that having all this data will allow us salespeople to better target our sales efforts."

"That's what I'm afraid of, Marcos," said Paul, with more than a little stress in his voice. "As these targeting efforts become more refined and personalized, where is there an opportunity for us salespeople to get involved and add the human touch?"

"That's a valid concern," answered Marcos. "Both customers and salespeople have realized that many elements of the sales process can be handled effectively virtually or digitally. Many customer surveys that were conducted both during and shortly after the pandemic indicated a preference for limited, and in some surveys zero, personal contact between the customer and the salesperson."

"I've seen those results and, in some cases, experienced those preferences," said Paul with more than a touch of exasperation in his voice. "So is the importance of the human touch going to continue to be diminished?"

Marcos gave him the trademark TBS smile. "What subsequent research has found," he said, "is that a number of those dire predictions did not fully materialize. We've found that customers have and will continue to seek the input of a salesperson. However, what B2B marketers and salespeople need to understand is that the definition of the human touch needs to be expanded. We traditionally think of the human touch as face-to-face interaction. Remember that Lydia James mentioned some research that found that B2B customers will engage with their vendors between five and seven times during the course of their purchase journey. Other research found that even though a significant percentage of B2B buyers said they would prefer having no contact with a sales representative, those who completed a self-service digital commerce purchase with no salesperson assistance are about one and a half times more likely to regret a purchase than buyers whose purchase was facilitated by a salesperson. Also, B2B buyers are almost twice as likely to complete a high-quality purchase when they employ supplier-provided digital tools in partnership with a salesperson. Finally, when a salesperson assisted in providing digital purchasing pathways for their customers, buyer regret was half of self-service purchases."

"Okay, I get that there's still a place for us as salespeople to add the human touch during the sales journey," Paul said. "But how do we combine all the digital data we have about the customer with providing the human touch?"

"Let me ask you a question," Marcos said. "Put yourself in the role of one of your customers. You're making an important purchase and are seeking assistance or critical information from your vendor during a certain stage of the buying journey. Who would you want that information to come from, an electronic source or a live person?"

The Weaving Process

"A live person, of course."

"And who are you going to trust more?"

"I see where you're going with this."

"What we've discovered here at Bickerton is that to be effective in providing the human touch we must use the process of *weaving*. We weave together the activities and benefits of both the digital and human interactions to create as cohesive a level of assistance to the customer as possible. We continue to emphasize to our salespeople the importance of remaining in contact with our customers throughout their purchase journey and responding immediately and accurately to their requests. We've also designed and provided access to digital information and tools to allow our salespeople to assist our customers during their purchase journey. At the same time, we continue to focus on making ourselves available to provide the human touch whenever and however our customers desire it. The more ways we can make ourselves available to provide the human touch, the more opportunities we have to build trust into the relationship."

Social Proof

Marcos hesitated, and Paul could tell he was thinking about what he wanted to talk about next.

"Now, let's talk about another important consideration regarding how we can build trust through the human touch and show our consistency at the same time," Marcos said. "We tend to think of the human touch as coming from one-on-one, usually face-to-face, contact with the salesperson. However, let's expand our thinking a bit. Think for a moment. Who else besides salespeople could create the human touch with our customers?"

"I never really thought about that," answered Paul. After thinking for a moment, his face lit up. "Of course! Other customers giving recommendations," he exclaimed.

"There you go," answered Marcos. "The study on trust I mentioned earlier found that the institutions or groups of people that B2B buyers trust most are the coworkers and management within their own companies, current and former customers, industry peers and analysts, and vendors they currently work with. On the other side of the coin are social media influencers, government officials, the news media, and unfortunately vendor salespeople have the least amount of trust.

The groups that B2B buyers trust most are the coworkers and management within their own companies, current and former customers, industry peers and analysts, and their current vendors.

"Ideally, what we'd like to have is a *chorus of voices* coming from sources that customers already trust saying reinforcing and positive things about us as a vendor," Marcos continued. "This is what is known as the principle of *social proof*. Research has found that only about 5 percent of people are initiators and the other 95 percent are imitators.

If one of the sources that your customers already trust advocates for you, it will have a *far* greater impact than any information we can offer. Therefore, we as vendors must make a concerted effort to involve the sources that our buyers already trust to communicate directly to those customers that we would like to directly influence. Having some quotes, reviews, or testimonials from influential people in the industry or community really helps to transform your relationship into a more trusting one."

> ## The Principle of Social Proof
>
> **If one of the sources that your customers already trust advocates for you, it will have a far greater impact than any information you can offer.**

"Interesting," said Paul. "And it would seem that not only could these other sources positively influence our customers, but they could also help mitigate some of their perceived risk and make them less likely to take a defensive position."

"Absolutely!" said Marcos. "So, the wider the footprint we can create in the marketplace, the more we are building the influence of ourselves and our products. And this influence combined with the three trust levers that B2B buyers say are most important could really have a positive impact on their purchase decision."

Summarizing Building the Trust

Marcos and Paul sat back in their chairs at the same time.

"Whew," said Marcos, "we covered a lot of territory in a pretty short period of time. So, what are your takeaways from our discussion?"

"Well," said Paul, "once again I see how the Pillars of being a Serving Salesperson build on each other. By setting serving as your true north, you lay the groundwork for the other Pillars. In regard to building trust through the human touch, I learned that knowing the Seven Levers of Trust, especially competence, consistency, and dependability, has given me insight as to what priorities I need to set and behaviors I need to practice going forward. Also, combining this with the credible sources our customer trusts will help us transform our relationship with them."

"You know we're not done with you, don't you?" said Marcos with a smile. "As has been the case with the other Pillars, there are some exercises for you to complete. I look forward to meeting with you in a few weeks to see what you've come up with."

Paul rose out of his chair and extended his hand. "Thank you very much for your insight. It's been true pleasure talking and learning from you."

"It's been my pleasure, Paul," said Marcos accepting Paul's hand with a firm grip and his ever-present smile. "And I look forward to seeing you in a few weeks to learn how you've incorporated building trust into your sales approach."

A Trust-Building Opportunity

Driving back to the office Paul had already begun to think about how he was going to employ what he'd learned about how to build trust through the human touch.

It had taken him several attempts over a few months to schedule an appointment for the next week with William Allen, the chief design engineer for North American Manufacturing. One of NAM's three large facilities was about an hour away from Petra. Paul managed to get his appointment by developing a relationship with Cheryl, William's administrative assistant. After several conversations with Cheryl, Paul had learned that both his and her families had vacationed on the North Carolina shore and shared a common love for the ocean and the area. Over the next few months, Paul kept trying to get on Willam's calendar. Finally, two weeks ago Cheryl found a thirty-minute appointment for

Paul and said, "That's the only open slot he has for three weeks." Paul suspected she was doing him a favor and was grateful for the opportunity. Now he knew he had to make the most of that opportunity.

Background Research

All Paul knew about William was that he went by William and was NAM's chief design engineer. He also had heard that NAM used some components in their manufacturing process similar to those that Petra made, but he wasn't sure. He figured those components were supplied by one of Petra's competitors, but he didn't know who. He had some work to do.

Paul set about gathering information about NAM and its industry. After returning to the office, he asked Cambrie, a recent college graduate, to help him do some research on NAM. Paul watched as Cambrie's fingers flew over the keyboard and was amazed at what she was able to find about NAM in a very short period. In just a few minutes Cambrie was able to pull up several recent articles and industry reports on NAM. She was also able to find some online profiles for William that gave information on him and his background. Paul was so impressed he ordered Cambrie's lunch to be delivered. He then spent much of the rest of the day reading and digesting the new information.

At home that evening Paul re-read and summarized the information he had received. He began to think about how he could illustrate to both William and NAM his and Petra's competence, consistency, and dependability. He began making a list of the things he could do, the examples he could use, and the stories and customer testimonials he could pull together that would demonstrate those three key capabilities.

He discovered that one of NAM's main competitors was a customer of Petra's. He quickly found the salesperson that was dealing with that customer and asked her to contact him at her earliest convenience. The next day he had a phone conversation with her and got some valuable information on both NAM and their competitors.

The articles Cambrie had found also referred to some technological advancements and pending legislation that were occurring in NAM's industry that could conceivably have an impact on NAM's manufacturing process. Paul then had conversations with Petra's engineering and legal departments and learned some valuable information to include in his presentation.

Finally, by perusing through social media he was able to learn about William's background—where he had gone to college and some management development seminars he had both attended and taught. He had also written a trade magazine article and couple of blog posts on one of NAM's manufacturing innovations. There was even a social media post about his daughter's college graduation. With all this new information he felt he had a pretty good handle on William, NAM, and its industry.

At the office the next morning Paul thought about the chorus of voices Marcos had mentioned and how they could speak positively about Petra's products and him as well. He thought of three key customers for whom he had recently resolved some significant issues. The first person he called was Neil Todd, who he had driven through the snow to help and then recommended a competitor to solve their problem. Neil picked up the phone on the second ring.

"Well, hello, Paul. To what do I owe the pleasure of this call?"

"Hi, Neil, I was hoping you would be willing to assist me by providing some information to a prospective customer."

Paul then contacted the people at Petra who handled their social media to find out what positive comments or reviews Petra had received and the best way to allow both William and NAM to access them. Finally, he was able to combine some of the information on advances in the industry with some product advancements Petra had made recently and put up his own social media post about how Petra had applied these advancements. With all this newfound information Paul set about preparing for his call with William.

Finishing with Marcos

Finding himself back at Bickerton Industrial Supply at the end of the month, Marcos paged through Paul's journal, smiling and nodding approvingly as he read each entry. Finally, he looked up and asked, "So, what happened at your appointment with North American Manufacturing?"

Paul had a beaming smile on his face. "It went far better than expected," he said. "As I was not the incumbent salesperson, I knew that I was going to have to establish that I was coming from a position of trust. To accomplish this, I did some research and got a good handle on their market and who their main competitors are. I was also able to discover which of my competitors' products NAM was using and could then discuss some of the issues other customers have been having with those products. I asked two of my customers to record short videos of the issues that I had resolved for them and sent William the links. I also sent him a link to our customer reviews."

"Wow!" said Marcos. "That had to set the stage pretty well, didn't it?"

"I'll get to that in a minute," Paul said. "I began my presentation by first asking William what it was like to have a daughter graduating from college. I told him I have two girls and wanted to know how I could get them there! That got him to laugh and broke the ice.

"William began the conversation by saying how impressed he was with Neil Todd's testimonial and that I had driven almost two hours through sloppy weather only to recommend a competitor's product. He said he had never had a salesperson do that in all his years of dealing with salespeople. I was then able to steer the conversation around to ask how they were dealing with issues in the industry that I had learned about and then segued into whether they were having issues with the specific products I was there to talk about.

"Marcos, I came in with an understanding of the industry, their market, and some of their issues. That, combined with my customers' testimonials and company reviews, provided a nice package of illustrating my and my company's competence, consistency, and dependability.

It helped me establish that both Petra and I could be trusted and helped to begin the process of really transforming the relationship."

"So, what happened?" asked Marcos.

"My half-hour sales call turned into an hour and a half as William canceled his next meeting. He then took me through the plant and showed me the products they were having trouble with. He referenced that by reading the information I had sent to him he had learned some of our products had had success in similar situations. Now we have a team going there in two weeks to conduct a product trial on their equipment. If it goes how I feel it will, I'm pretty confident that it could open the door for a significant opportunity."

Marcos smiled a broad smile. "You've learned well, Paul, and have really shown by your actions that you have a good understanding of how to build trust through the human touch. Titus 2:7-8 says, 'In everything set them an example by doing what is good. In your teaching show integrity, seriousness and soundness of speech that cannot be condemned.' It truly sounds like you're prepared to build trust through the human touch with your customers. You are ready to go on to Phoebe Andrews to learn about Pillar Five: Communicate for Impact. I'll let her know you'll be contacting her soon. I've enjoyed our time together, Paul, and I look forward to seeing you again.

"Well done!"

Pillar Five
Communicate for Impact

*To effectively communicate, we must realize that we are
all different in the way we perceive the world and use this
understanding as a guide to our communication with others.*

— Tony Robbins

**Communicate for
Impact**

Confrontation in the Garage

The day after Paul finished with Marcos Simón was a warm, sunny Saturday at the end of March. As often happens on the first warm day after a long winter, Paul felt the need to be outside, to enjoy the nice weather and to get his mind around all he had been learning. He would have loved to have taken his girls on the drive, but they were off with their mother visiting Mary's parents.

After driving around rather aimlessly thinking about his interviews, Paul found himself in his old neighborhood and on the street that until about a year ago he had called home. As he drove past his house, he couldn't help but notice that the yard was in desperate need of some clean-up from the winter. Paul had always taken great pride in the curb appeal of his house, and he was suddenly overcome by a sense of remorse and guilt, coming to realize yet another repercussion of his selfish act of moving out.

Suddenly and without thinking, Paul turned into the driveway and got out of the car. Even though he didn't have a key to the house anymore (fallout from him leaving in such a huff), he discovered that the code on the keypad to the garage door was the same as it had always been—the date of their wedding. Pulling on his old work gloves and finding some trash bags, he set about cleaning out the garage before tackling the work outside.

After a few minutes Paul sensed something behind him and whirled around to find his next-door neighbor Nathan Brown standing there with a rather surprised look on his face.

"Oh, hello, Paul. I'm rather surprised to see you here. We knew that Mary and the kids were gone, and I was just—"

"No need to explain, Nathan. I'm probably the last person you expected to see. I hadn't planned on coming over. I was just driving by and saw all the work that needed to be done in the yard."

Nathan eyed Paul suspiciously. While Mary and Susan, Nathan's wife, had a good relationship and attended a Bible study together, Paul and Nathan had barely had any relationship at all. Paul's interactions with Nathan had pretty much been limited to things like complaining to him about things like their barking dog or their kids leaving their toys in his yard. Looking at Nathan, Paul was suddenly overcome with a sense of embarrassment and even shame that he had always been so rude to him.

"Well, Paul, I guess I'll be going now that I know it's you," said Nathan, turning and starting to walk away.

"Nathan," Paul called after him. Nathan half turned around and looked at Paul.

"I'm sorry."

"Come again?"

"I'm sorry, Nathan, sorry for the way I've treated you and your family. I'm sorry that the only conversations we ever seemed to have were when I was complaining to you about things that neighbors shouldn't complain to each other about. I'm sorry that I know virtually nothing about you, Susan, or your kids. I'm sorry for being such a total jerk the whole time you've lived here, and I hope you'll forgive me."

Nathan was now fully turned back toward Paul and stared at him in stunned silence, not knowing what to say.

Paul continued. "I've been meeting with several people who are mentoring me on how to become a Serving Salesperson. While their knowledge and advice have helped me be a better salesperson, it's helped me in lots of other ways too. It's made me realize that we really are put here to serve others, and that by truly serving others we end up serving ourselves and gaining a level of satisfaction far better than when we focus only on serving ourselves."

Nathan now walked toward Paul. His look of suspicion turned into a friendly smile. "Tell me more about what you've learned, Paul," he said softly.

Nathan stood silently while Paul told him about his interviews and experiences. Nathan listened intently with a sincere look in his eyes.

After Paul had finished, Nathan hesitated and then began to speak.

Love Is a Verb

"Paul, just in these few short minutes I can tell you are a changed man," he said. "I guess you could say that this 'Serving Salesperson' mindset has carried over into your personal life and now you're serving Mary by doing some things that she can't get to."

Paul could only nod slightly in silent agreement.

"You know," Nathan began slowly, "maybe it's not my place to say this, but I feel I must. Things have been a lot different around here since you moved out. Because Mary had to go back to work, she and Susan haven't been able to do many of the things they used to do together."

Paul's chin dropped down onto his chest. Hearing the hard truth and looking Nathan in the eyes at the same time was just too difficult.

Nathan continued, his voice sharpening. "However, it goes a lot deeper than her just not having the time to do the things she used to do. You hurt her, Paul; you hurt her deeply, and it has caused her to withdraw from a lot of her friends and the things she used to enjoy. Hearing you now, it sounds like you're realizing the toll that your selfish attitude and self-centeredness had on your entire family."

Paul looked up. Nathan's piercing gaze bored right through him.

"I had that coming, Nathan, and I'm realizing that increasingly all the time. I've really been working hard to turn our relationship around, to get her to trust me again, to gain the love back that we once had," Paul said, putting his chin back on his chest again. He suddenly lifted his head and blurted out, "Do you think we can get it back, Nathan—that love we once had? Do you think she'll ever trust me again?"

"Paul, anything is possible. I know that Mary's Bible study group has been praying for just such a reconciliation, and a lot of other people, including me, are praying for the same thing. Mark 9:23 says, 'Everything is possible for one who believes,' and if you try hard enough and believe hard enough, good things are bound to happen."

Paul found that he was not at all put off by Nathan's comments—in fact he was encouraged by them. He then burst out, "Would you keep praying, Nathan? And tell me, what else can I do to win her back?"

Nathan just smiled. "Yes, I will, Paul, and you need to love her, love her and serve her."

"But I do love her, Nathan. I have deep feelings for her."

Nathan responded, "When I talk about loving her, I mean with an *agape* love, where love is a verb."

"What do you mean 'love is a verb'?"

"In the Greek language there are several different words to describe the many facets of love. The Greeks used the noun *agape* and the corresponding verb *agapao* to describe a *behavior,* an act of unconditional love toward others regardless of whether you feel they deserve it. Agape love means that no matter how I *feel* about others, I *behave* with a kind and loving spirit. That's what we're talking about here, Paul. It's more than feelings. It's love that is expressed through your behavior and actions toward others. To truly love Mary with an agape love means loving her and serving her through intentional actions, words, and deeds."

"But what if that doesn't work?" questioned Paul.

"Oh, I feel certain it will work," Nathan said with a friendly smile. Putting his hand on Paul's shoulder he continued, "And from what I can gather, deep down inside Mary still loves you, and true love does not allow failure to be final."

Halfway out of the garage, Nathan turned around. "By the way," he called out, "you can treat your customers with agape love as well."

Paul spent the rest of the day happily clipping, raking, sweeping, and bagging. Other than an hour's break for a soup and sandwich dinner with Nathan and Susan, he worked until almost dark.

Before he left Paul knocked on the Browns' back door to thank them for dinner and to say goodbye. As he reached out to shake Nathan's hand, Nathan eschewed his outstretched hand and embraced him in a bro hug. "Remember to keep making love a verb," he whispered in Paul's ear. Much to his surprise Susan hugged him as well. "Know that I'm going to be praying extra hard for both of you," she whispered.

A Surprise Visit

Sunday evening around dinnertime Paul was jolted from his reading by the ringing of his apartment doorbell. Looking out the front door window, he saw Mary and the girls holding what looked like a pizza box. He also could hear his little dachshunds, Gracie and Alex, at their feet, barking with excitement. While seeing his girls made him happy, seeing his wife made his stomach turn somersaults. He couldn't open the door fast enough.

"Thank you *so much*, Daddy, for making our house look so nice," said Elizabeth, as the dogs happily jumped up to greet him.

"Yeah, thanks, Daddy," added Ruthie. "Now our house looks the best of any of the houses on our street!"

"You really didn't have to do that, Paul," said Mary, who suddenly found it difficult to look into his eyes. "But I really appreciate it," she said, putting the pizza box down and reaching out and giving him a hug. Even through her jacket she felt good to Paul. It had been a long time since she had hugged him.

The evening went by all too quickly, and with it being a school night Mary and the girls needed to head home. Paul stopped Mary on her way out.

"Mary, I was wondering ... would you consider letting me ... I mean—"

"Oh, Paul, please don't ask me. I'm just not ready for that yet. I hear you talking about how you've changed, and it's been nice spending more time with you. And what you did this weekend was really sweet. But you hurt me deeply, and that hurt has not totally gone away. I like the changes I see in you and I'm working to trust you again, but I'm just not there yet."

Paul watched them drive away, the girls waving out their windows and holding Gracie and Alex up to the window and waving their paws to say goodbye. That lonely, empty feeling returned.

He slowly shut the door.

Communicate for Impact

A few mornings later in the first week of April Paul was sitting in the office of Phoebe Andrews, a partner in a sales training and marketing consulting firm. Her office was warm yet professional, almost homey. Phoebe was a tall, slender African American woman in her mid-forties who moved with the poise and grace of a former dancer that Paul had learned she was. She was clearly very bright as she had both her undergraduate and master's degrees in psychology as well as her MBA. As with other members of the TBS, Phoebe was friendly, outgoing, very successful, and above all anxious to assist Paul on his journey to becoming a Serving Salesperson.

After exchanging some pleasantries, Phoebe began the conversation with, "Tell me Paul, what have you learned so far?" Paul responded with his now-familiar tale of how meeting with the previous members of the TBS had not only changed his method of selling but his entire outlook on life.

"Paul, I had a nice conversation with Marcos Simón. He was impressed with how far you came in your time with him."

"Not half as much as I was impressed with him," Paul responded softly.

"Well, my task is to talk with you about the fifth Pillar of being a Serving Salesperson: Communicate for Impact," Phoebe said. "And if we're going to have impactful communication, we have to focus on using brain-friendly communication. If we understand how the brain gathers, processes, and retains information we are going to be able to have much more impactful communication. Shall we begin?"

"Gosh, Phoebe," said Paul." "If we are going to talk about how the brain functions, you're probably going to have go slow. I'm afraid the physical sciences have never really been my strong suit. I'm familiar with the whole 'left brain-right brain' concept, but other than that I'm clueless."

"Not to worry, Paul," said Phoebe flashing that knowing smile that seemed to be the trademark of the TBS members. "My interest in this field came about because of my desire to apply the principles of psychology to sales. My partners and I continue to search for ways we can use that information to assist our clients to communicate for impact.

"What we've learned from our research was instrumental in establishing this Pillar. But we're not going to get too far down in the weeds of the physiology of how the brain works. Our focus is to give you enough of an understanding of how the brain works to assist you to communicate for impact. At this point you have laid a solid foundation for transforming the relationship with your customer by setting serving as your true north, blending passion and perseverance, sharpening your EQ, and building trust through the human touch. The next step is to combine what you've learned about these Pillars and to be able to communicate for impact."

Phoebe settled back in her chair with an introspective look on her face. "Let's start with a simple question," she said. "What's your main objective in a sales call?"

Paul answered immediately, "To advance the sale forward to reach the point where the customer will purchase your product."

"And how do you accomplish that?"

Again, a quick answer from Paul: "By influencing their thinking to the point where they determine that the benefits they will receive from our product are greater than the benefits they will receive from any competitive product and the benefits can justify the price."

"You just said a key phrase, Paul, *influence their thinking*. Let's dive deeper into that. How do you gain influence with your customers to the point where it will impact their thinking not only about your product but about you as well?"

"I've never given much thought about how you gain influence," Paul said. "I guess I thought it came about because of your positive actions over time."

"You're getting there, Paul. A key factor in communicating for impact is to be able to *influence* a customer's thinking by bringing them around to your point of view. And there are two ways you can influence a customer."

Dominance and Prestige

Phoebe leaned forward and continued, "To gain influence you can either *establish* dominance or *earn* prestige. What do those two terms mean to you?"

Paul paused for a minute before answering. "I would say that establishing dominance means that a person gains influence because they portray themselves as being powerful and authoritative. They would also use forceful communication and to convince customers that they and their products are superior."

> *There are two ways you can influence a customer: You can either establish dominance or earn prestige.*

"Now, how do you think most B2B customers react to a salesperson trying to establish dominance?"

"Not very well I would think."

"That's right," Phoebe replied. "Not surprisingly, a skeptical audience reacts very negatively to a dominant approach. And can your audiences be skeptical?"

"When are they not?" Paul asked.

"Now," Phoebe said, "how does a person earn prestige?"

"By engaging in all the behaviors that a Serving Salesperson exhibits, being honest and forthright in your dealings with others and focusing on understanding your customer's needs."

"And which do you suppose is the most productive path to earning prestige?" Phoebe asked.

"Let me guess. Is it by being a Serving Salesperson and communicating for impact?"

Phoebe smiled. "Earning prestige is a key to positively influencing your customer and also factors in if we're going to transform the relationship with our customers," she said. "Let's talk about how we can go about earning prestige."

Two Systems

Phoebe leaned forward in her chair and began. "We have two systems in our brain that work together to process information. Notice we use the term *systems* rather than *brains* because there are several bodily functions both inside and outside the brain that become involved, depending on the type of decision our brain is faced with. We're going to go into more detail than the left brain-right brain terminology and instead refer to the *reflective system* and the *reactive system*. If we're going to be successful in transforming our relationship with the customer, we have to have an understanding of how both systems work.

"When faced with making a decision, the reactive system will be the first to kick in. The reactive system is part of the brain's limbic system, which is emotionally driven and makes intuitive, unconscious, lightning-fast, gut-level type decisions.

"The reflective system, on the other hand, operates in a slower, more rational, more calculating manner. It's this system that handles things like reading the small print on a legal document, filling out your tax return, being able to decipher the latest new product information."

Phoebe continued, "One of the key features of the human brain is its ability to combine these two decision-making systems together. This dual decision-making capacity allows for speed, accuracy, and efficient energy consumption."

Paul looked up and interrupted. "Energy consumption?" he asked.

"Yes," replied Phoebe. "If you give me just a minute, I'll get to that."

"Sorry for the interruption," replied Paul rather sheepishly.

"Now, here's the catch," Phoebe said, digging back in. "When making a decision, the rational, calculating reflective system kicks in anywhere from a half-second to a few seconds slower than the more emotional reactive system. Plus—and here's a key point—the thinking, reflective system also consumes more mental energy and tires out rapidly."

"So, is this where the energy consumption part comes in?" asked Paul.

"Absolutely," answered Phoebe. "Our digestive system converts the food we eat into glucose, which is the fuel our bodies and brains run on. The brain is the hungriest organ in the human body and consumes 20 to 25% of the glucose the body produces. However, the brain never knows how much glucose it's going to have available at any given time. Therefore, to save energy, the brain first will engage the reactive system in a gut-level decision-making process. The reactive system burns far less glucose and in effect becomes the default setting when your brain is in energy conservation mode."

System Personalities

Phoebe continued. "Now I'm going to attach personal descriptions to each of these systems to hopefully describe them better. Think of the reflective system as the boring, buttoned-up accountant that scrutinizes every number on the page, every cell in the spreadsheet, every line on the balance sheet. They operate in a logical, analytical, and methodical manner. Let me give you an example of how the reflective system works. When you get your company's medical coverage document for the year, do you read and digest the entire thing in one sitting?"

Paul smiled and shook his head. "I lose my focus trying to process all the information before I've finished the second page."

"That's because of the mental energy it took to process that information—you've tired out your reflective system. Now let's switch over to the reactive system. Let's use an unpredictable college roommate as an example. Did you have one of those?"

Paul smiled as a few of his college fraternity brothers came to mind.

"I'm guessing by the smile on your face you've thought of someone," Phoebe said. "As we discussed, emotions are at the core of reactive decision-making. The reactive system is quick, impulsive, and intuitive, and here's where the system part comes in. Emotions such as happiness, excitement, fear, anger, and disgust all trigger the release of chemicals in the brain that are associated with each emotion. I'm going to mention some of these chemicals here and then talk about them in more detail when we discuss storytelling."

Paul stopped his notetaking and looked up. "So, how does this happen?" he said.

"As a salesperson we especially need to understand the impact that negative emotions have on decision making. Self-preservation is a very strong instinct in all living things, and the reactive system controls the 'fight or flight' reactions of the brain," Phobe said. "This has led to us as humans developing a strong fear of loss. This fear of loss is still present today such that the fear of loss is more than twice as powerful as the possibility of gain. This leads to having more negative neural networks in the brain, which a salesperson needs to be aware of."

Understanding Threat Networks

"Now, here's a very key factor that enters into dealing with the fear of loss and the defensive posture buyers take," Phoebe said. "As I just mentioned, there are more negative threat networks than positive networks in the reactive system. If a salesperson expects to be successful in influencing customers to advance the sale forward, they first need to understand that these threat networks exist and second to work to overcome the negative impact of these networks. If we're going to really transform the relationship with our customer, we have to account for how these threat networks can influence that perspective."

Phoebe paused for a moment to make sure she had Paul's full attention. "Having to overcome the effect of these threat networks is why it's very important for us as Serving Salespeople to *earn prestige* with our customers by bringing the principles of the Seven Pillars into play. Bringing in the principles of the Seven Pillars will allow us to connect emotionally with our customers and help us to override those negative threat networks present in the reactive system. That's why coming in with a dominant style stands very little chance of success. The emotional connection with the reactive system needs to be established first."

A Serving Salesperson needs to work to overcome
the negative impact of the threat networks in the brain.

"Gosh, Phoebe," Paul said, I really had no knowledge of how the reactive system works. This is going to be tremendously helpful going forward."

Phoebe smiled. "That's a lot to take in in one sitting," she said. "How about a short break before we continue?"

Phoebe brought back two cups of coffee. They sat and relaxed for a bit while enjoying their drinks. Paul was even more intrigued to learn more about the topic.

Emotions and Decision-Making

Phoebe started up again. "Let's now focus on understanding emotions and decisions making," said Phoebe. "Salespeople need to understand how the various emotions individuals experience during the decision process engage the limbic elements of the reactive system," she began. "Different types of emotions will activate certain parts of the brain which in turn will release certain chemicals that can impact that individual's behavior. We know that there is a link between the emotion of happiness and the part of the brain that releases dopamine. Dopamine is sometimes referred to as brain candy and is called the happy hormone because it allows us to feel pleasure, satisfaction, and even motivation.

"On the other side of the equation, situations that involve negative emotions, such as fear, anger, or disgust, unlock the brain's amygdala region and trigger the chemicals associated with fear—cortisol and adrenaline. The amygdala sends signals to the part of the brain that controls heart rate, blood pressure, respiration patterns, gut contractions, and a host of other negative reactions. These reactions in turn will cause us to feel stress."

"Wow! This is really interesting stuff," Paul said, "but when does the logical system get involved?"

"Good question, Paul," Phoebe answered. "It's essential to understand that emotions are at the core of the reactive system's emotional decision making. In the faster, in-the-moment decision-making, the reflective system's logical mental processes take a back seat to the reactive system. Because the reflective system operates a few seconds slower, it can kick in after the decision is made and can sometimes serve to help us rationalize the decision. Research has shown that people often feel their way into making a decision and then rationalize it afterward. This speaks to the importance of creating positive emotions for the brain to store.

"Okay, we now need to talk about how we can create positive memories for our customers," Phoebe said.

Creating Positive Memories

"Humans have a three-process approach to storing memory. Scientists refer to these processes as short-term memory, working memory, and long-term memory. We're going to focus on how the short-term and long-term memories work together to retain information.

"When new information is introduced to your brain it goes into your short-term memory, which holds that information for only about twenty to thirty seconds. Think of the short-term memory as a video camera that runs continuously recording little snippets of information and then records over them almost immediately. We know that your brain decides to retain some of these snippets, and neuroscientists have postulated that your brain retains those that are considered to be the most relevant at the time. These retained snippets then get uploaded into your long-term memory storage for further consideration and application down the road.

"Now, here's a key point for us as salespeople," continued Phoebe. "We know that the short-term memory has the capacity to process and retain only two or three bits of information at a time. So, let me ask you a question, Paul. How might that affect how we present information on our products to our customer?"

Paul thought for a minute. "That means if we give them a long list of the features of our products, it's probably going to overwhelm the capacity of the short-term memory."

"So, what information should we focus on presenting to the customer?"

"The information that's going to be more important to them in making the product decision."

"And how do we find that out?"

"By asking them," Paul said with a sigh.

Let me give you an acronym to use with your customers," said Phoebe.

"Let's hear it."

"WIMITY."

"What?"

"WIMITY. That stands for **W**hat **I**s the **M**ost **I**mportant **T**hing to **Y**ou? What are they going to tell you when you ask them that?"

"What's most important to them."

"And what's the next question you ask?"

Paul smiled "Why is that important to you?"

WIMITY

What

Is the

Most

Important

Thing to

You?

"And then what did you learn from Lydia James about asking questions that you could apply here?"

"Peel the onion," Paul said. "Peel the onion down a couple of layers to discover the two or three points of our product that are most important to them and why they believe those points will create more benefits than what they have now."

"That's right," said Phoebe. "So, the task for Serving Salespeople is to ask the customer the WIMITY question early on and then peel the onion to discover the two or three features that are most important to them. We then can focus on demonstrating how our product will fulfill their needs and thus create positive emotions for that product. If we're successful in doing that, we can help the customer transfer the information from their short-term memory and 'assign' it as positive information in their long-term memory."

The Serving Salesperson needs to ask the WIMITY question and then peel the onion to discover the two or three features that are the most important to the customer.

"And how does that help them remember that information?"

Again, Paul smiled and said, "By hopefully transferring those two or three bits of information from the short-term memory into the long-term memory."

"Now, one more bit of information to save for later," Phoebe said. "Peeling the onion offers an opportunity to begin to initiate the first phase of guiding the customer to transform themselves: helping them to discover what possibilities might exist. Here you can begin to ask the customers what their ideal solution might be and what obstacles are preventing them from getting to that solution. John Philips will discuss this more when you talk with him about how to guide the transformation."

"A question, Phoebe," Paul asked. "How can we activate these strong emotions in our customers' brains if our products aren't that exciting?"

Phoebe smiled and said, "Your products by themselves probably aren't going to create powerful emotions. However, the *benefits* that they've created for other customers can. Like Marcos Simón talked about, we need to craft our presentations to create a more *positive experience* for our customers. For example, we can employ that chorus of voices Marcos mentioned and get previous customers to talk about the value that your product created for them. You can also take advantage of the social proof that Marcos Simón mentioned in his discussions with you. You can then build on what others have said by painting a picture in their mind, a picture that will get them thinking about how they can have the same success. And the best way to create that mental picture for them is by storytelling, relating how your product solved a similar problem for another customer."

Storytelling

"There's a lot of research around the value of storytelling in persuasive communication," said Phoebe with that knowing smile, "and storytelling is one of the most effective ways to communicate for impact. Let's talk about the impact that storytelling has on the brain and how a salesperson can use it to their advantage.

"The first advantage that storytelling offers is what has been termed *neural coupling*. Research has shown that storytelling synchronizes the brain activity of the listener with the brain activity of the storyteller. Studies have found that as a story was being told, the listener's brain responses became coupled to the storyteller's brain responses. What happens is that the story activates the parts in the listener's brain that allows them to turn the story into their own ideas and experience. They in effect imagine themselves as part of the story which then draws them into that story."

Storytelling activates the parts of the listener's brain that allows them to turn the story into their own experience and draw them into the story.

Phoebe continued, "The next effect storytelling has on the brain is *cortex activity*. Stories activate parts of the brain that regulate the emotions, motivations, and beliefs of the reactive system of the listener, as we discussed earlier. There are the three chemical substances that telling a story activates within the brain.

"The first is *cortisol*. Think of cortisol as nature's built-in alarm system. It works with certain parts of your brain to control an individual's mood, motivation, and fear. When cortisol is released, it tells the brain 'Listen up! Something important is about to happen here.' You can activate the release of cortisol by making an attention-getting statement, asking a question, or describing a situation that will engage your audience.

"Next is *dopamine*, the brain candy I mentioned earlier. When the listener hears a positive emotionally charged story, the brain releases excess dopamine which activates the brain's learning systems. This in turn allows the listener to experience arousal or pleasure. Dopamine will help the listener remember the facts of the story and remember those facts with greater accuracy."

Phoebe paused to take a drink and then continued. "And the third substance is *oxytocin*—the same chemical that floods a mother's body after the birth of her child," she said. "To produce this chemical an individual will need to tell stories that tug at the heartstrings and will appeal to the customer's emotions. Inspiring the listener to produce oxytocin is the key to evoking empathy in the listener and will help the listener to trust you more."

Engage with Storytelling

Phoebe sat back in her chair and paused for a moment.

"Paul, I think we'd both agree that the best salespeople are the best storytellers. We've talked about the chemical reactions that are going on in the brain when a story is being told. Now let's talk about four key elements that help to make the story memorable—a descriptive setting, vivid and identifiable characters, an object of desire, and obstacles. I'm going to go down these bullet points that list the four elements that every story should include and talk about how you can make each element memorable for your audience."

- *A Descriptive Setting.* Crafting a memorable descriptive setting is a powerful storytelling tool to transport the audience into the world of the narrative. Three key factors can be used here—stage, mood, and meaning:
  - Stage—where does the story take place? What are the important physical details of the setting?
  - Mood—How does it feel? What emotions are present?
  - Meaning—Why does the setting matter? What is the symbolism and relevance to the plot or the characters?
- *Vivid and Identifiable Characters.* Characters are the heartbeat of any story and give it meaning. To make characters vivid and identifiable, a storyteller needs to blend detail, emotion, and relatability so the audience can *see* them, *hear* them, and also

remember them long after the story ends. Creating vivid and identifiable characters should include the following:

- o Appearance—What do they look like? What are their most memorable traits?
- o Voice—How do they sound? What do their dialogue, tone, and rhythm sound like?
- o Essence—What are they like inside? What are their values, motives, and fears?

- *An Object of Desire.* The object of desire is what drives the story. It's what its characters pursue, what drives conflict, and what keeps the audience invested. To make it memorable, you need to shape it with clarity, emotional weight, and symbolic resonance. A memorable object of desire should be:
  - o Tangible—What is it physically? Is it an object, a destination, a hopeful goal?
  - o Emotional—Why do characters crave it? Is it success, survival, redemption?
  - o Symbolic—What larger meaning does it carry? Power, faith, legacy?

- *Obstacles.* Obstacles are the lifeblood of storytelling. They create tension, test characters, and keep audiences engaged. A memorable obstacle isn't just a hurdle; it's a meaningful challenge that reveals character and deepens the story's themes. A memorable obstacle can be a:
  - o Barrier—What blocks the path? Is it physical, emotional, social, or spiritual?
  - o Choice—What decision must be made? Does the character fight, flee, compromise, or sacrifice?

"And one more thing," Phoebe added. "Researchers have found three factors that the brain stores in its memory that help people remember a story: vivid and identifiable characters, sensory imagery, and suspense."

Thankfully, Phoebe leaned back in her chair, signaling that Paul should relax as well.

"I know this has all come at you pretty fast," Phoebe replied. "In the files you've been provided there are some links to some more information. I'd recommend reviewing that information as it should help bring into focus what we've talked about today."

"Thank you very much, Phoebe. Again, this was very educational as well as downright fascinating. I'll see you at the end of the month."

"It's been my pleasure, Paul. Come, let me walk you out."

As Paul had experienced with the other members of the TBS, Phoebe sent him off with a warm handshake. "I've enjoyed our time together Paul, and I look forward to our next meeting and hearing about your progress."

It wasn't long before Paul found an opportunity to communicate for impact and put his knowledge of brain-friendly communication to use and communicate for impact.

A Communicate for Impact Opportunity

As Paul was reviewing his schedule for the upcoming week, he focused on an appointment with a mechanical engineer named Charlie Pritchard about providing some products for an upcoming project that Charlie's company was putting together. Charlie was very friendly, outgoing, and gregarious, and Paul's sales calls with him always went over the allotted time. Yet his engineering background and sharp analytical mind made him a very demanding customer. He insisted on understanding the specific details of Petra's products and how they would perform in the application that Charlie's company was designing. While Paul's meetings with Charlie had always gone well, he had yet to get over the hump in influencing Charlie to agree to a product trial.

As Paul reviewed his notes from his previous meetings he discovered he had concentrated almost exclusively on communicating all the technical specifications of the product and how his product would perform better than the competition. While Charlie was interested, he remained unconvinced. Paul needed to find a way to advance the sale forward.

As he thought about this appointment it suddenly struck him that he had been focused almost totally on appealing to Charlie's reflective system and had paid almost no attention to Charlie's reactive system. He knew his product's quality and test results spoke for themselves. What he needed to do was appeal more to Charlie's reactive system and he began to think how he could use what he learned about brain-friendly communication to communicate for more impact and transform Charlie's perspective.

He remembered that Cathy Perkins had been successful in selling the product he was presenting to Charlie to one of her customers. He went to see her and came away with enough details to be able to craft a convincing story. He had a setting, descriptions of buying group members, details about their objective, and the obstacles the company had with the issue they were facing. Cathy had even been able to get her customer to record a short testimonial illustrating how Petra's product had resolved an issue very similar to what Charlie's company was facing. Paul uploaded that video to his phone and began to craft a story around it.

After exchanging a few pleasantries with Charlie in his office and learning about his latest rock-hound excursion, Paul began his presentation in earnest.

"Charlie, in reviewing the notes from our last meeting I noticed that you had a couple of misgivings about whether our product would fit into your new system. Can you tell me more about those?"

Charlie went into more detail about those misgivings and a couple of new ones that Paul was not aware of.

"And what is the most important thing to you about the impact of the system's implementation?" Paul asked.

"Hmm, good question," Charlie said. He sat back in his chair and began to lay out his concerns. As Charlie was giving his answer, Paul peeled the onion with follow-up questions that got down to the heart of those concerns. When Charlie had finished Paul reiterated those concerns back to him and made sure there was nothing else that bothered Charlie.

Paul then asked one more question. "Charlie, what would an ideal outcome in this situation look like for you?" Charlie thought for a minute and then listed a few key considerations as well as concerns.

Paul sat back in his chair and said, "You know, Charlie, we had a customer over in Westfield that had a very similar situation and almost the same concerns that you have. Do you want to hear what we did for them?"

"That would be great," Charlie answered, sitting up straight.

"Well, here's what their situation was..." Paul then told his carefully constructed story. Charlie leaned forward as Paul continued telling the story. Charlie nodded and even gave some positive feedback. After Paul ended his story he asked, "Would you like to hear how the customer felt about this product's performance?"

"Yes, I would," Charlie said enthusiastically.

"I can do better than that," Paul said. "Let me show you." Paul pulled up the testimonial on his phone and simply said, "Let them tell you how well this product worked for them." He put his phone in front of Charlie and hit play. Charlie was immediately drawn into the video and watched with rapt attention until the testimonial was over. Paul concluded his presentation with, "So what are your thoughts now, Charlie?"

"My thoughts are that I want to schedule a product trial on our system here to see if it will work for us. How soon can we get that going?"

"Let me call our engineers and installation people."

Making Love a Verb

Paul was feeling great about his newfound success at work and was also inspired to make love a verb with his family. He began to call Mary more often with offers of help or simply to ask about her day. He would make time in his schedule to pick up the girls from school, dancing, or piano lessons. He also did some of the home maintenance at their house, much to the delight of his girls and to the relief of Mary. He quietly began to pay some of the bills and do some errands to take some pressure off Mary. He found that not only did he enjoy serving his family, but that he also got an intense sense of satisfaction by doing so.

Back with Phoebe

At the end of March Paul once again was sitting in Phoebe's office, watching her go through his notes and exercises. After a while she looked up with a satisfied look on her face and asked, "So tell me, Paul, how has what you learned about communicating for impact made you a better Serving Salesperson?"

"It's made me realize that I have spent way too much time appealing to the reflective system and not enough to the reactive system. I've also learned how important it is to earn and maintain prestige with your customers by building a trusting relationship and working to overcome the negative networks in their reflective system. I now start by asking the WIMITY question and then peeling the onion to begin the discovery part of the transformation process. I'm also learning to craft better stories to more fully engage their reactive system. If I do that, I feel that have truly served them and given them something that they aren't getting from anyone else."

"Paul, you've learned well, and I'm delighted to pass you on to Luke Roman to discuss Pillar Six: Facilitate the Journey. In the meantime, continue to seek to gain an understanding of how to use brain-friendly communication to positively influence your customer. As Proverbs 16:23 says 'A wise man's heart guides his mouth, and his lips promote instruction.'

"Well done!"

Facilitate the Journey

Sellers who listen to buyers carefully and then give them the missing ingredients—those are the ones that stand out.

– Deb Calvert

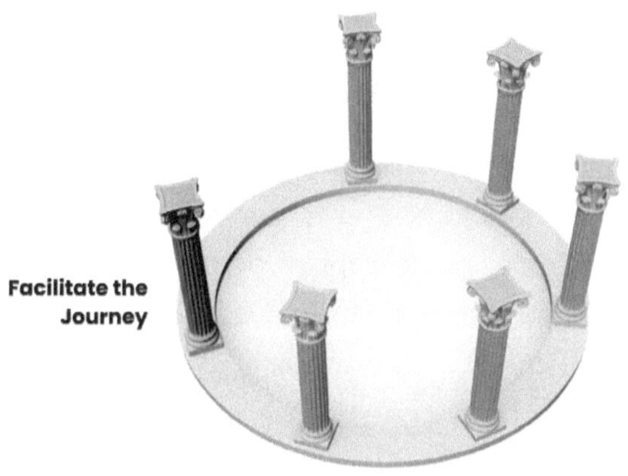

Effects of a Lost Sale

"PAUL RHODES TO see Luke Matthias."

It was the first week in April and Paul was in the office of Butler Incorporated, a large distributor of duplicating equipment where Luke Matthias was the sales manager. He had to admit he was a bit skeptical when he saw Luke's name on the list of the TBS people he was to interview. After all, his impression of copier salespeople was, shall we say, somewhat less than favorable. He had seen far too many of them troop through his office over the years, trying to hard-sell his company into switching over to their system. "We are so much better than what you have now," they'd say.

Paul heard footsteps coming down the hall. He turned to see a tall, trim, and athletic-looking gentleman in his early forties, impeccably dressed in a coat and tie and walking purposefully toward him.

"Good morning, Paul. I'm Luke Matthias. I've been looking forward to meeting you," Luke said extending his hand. He gave a firm handshake and exuded the confidence that Paul had also come to expect in a Serving Salesperson. "Let's go back to our conference room and get acquainted." Luke ushered Paul back to the office's conference room where they sat across the table from each other. After getting cups of coffee and exchanging a few pleasantries Luke said, "So tell me what you've learned so far about being a Serving Salesperson."

As Paul finished his story, Luke spoke up. "Your story certainly is consistent with what I've heard about you," he said. "We're all delighted to hear from Lew about how you've not only changed your approach to sales but how the entire concept of being a Serving Salesperson has begun to impact your whole life."

Lew? thought Paul. *Even Lew aware of what's been going on with me?*

"So, it's my job to talk to you about the next Pillar of being a Serving Salesperson: Facilitate the Journey. Let me begin by telling you why the TBS chose me to speak to you on this Pillar. Almost three years ago I lost what would have been the biggest sale of my career, one I was sure I was going to get. It would have made me the top salesperson for the year not only for our office but for all the distributor offices for the brand of duplicating equipment we sell. While I was disappointed, what upset me the most was that I thought I had done everything I needed to do to get the sale."

Even though this had happened some time ago it was clear that repeating the story had struck a nerve. Luke paused for a moment before continuing.

"A month after losing that big sale it was still eating at me, so I decided to try and find out why I'd lost it. I had developed a pretty good relationship with one of the guys in the buying group, so I sent him an email and asked if we could have a frank conversation as to why I lost the sale. To my surprise he agreed to a call that same afternoon."

"How did that go?" Paul asked.

"Humbling and sobering," said Luke with a sigh. "He was very up front and honest with me. Then he told me something that completely surprised me. He told me I just didn't seem to understand their needs, how they went about making purchasing decisions, and the information they needed to make their decision. He also said that it was a very complex purchase for them and the person who earned the sale had not only worked very hard to understand their needs, but was more helpful in guiding them through twists and turns of the purchase decision, and had provided them with critical information over and above what they asked for."

Luke paused for a moment and then continued, "As I thought about what the customer had said and reviewed my notes, I realized I had overlooked several things. I realized that I had made a lot of assumptions based on my prior experiences about how I *thought* the sale was going to progress. I also realized that for the first time in my career there were several people in the buying group that were younger than me. I just didn't recognize that as a group they simply approached the buying journey differently and had different priorities than I thought they had. I had to admit to myself that I really hadn't connected very well with them and what had been my time-honored way of selling to such groups just wasn't as effective as it used to be. I also learned that just sending your customers a bunch of product information isn't enough. You must make a concerted effort to make the information easy for them to understand and digest.

"What concerned me even more was that our sales team had talked about this as a group beforehand, and we all felt I was taking the right approach. That made me realize that not only did I not have a good understanding of how to sell successfully in this environment, but apparently most of our salespeople didn't either. Not only was I personally going to have to revise my sales approach, but if we were going to transform the relationship with our customers and attempt to shift their perspective, most of our salespeople were going to have to revise theirs as well."

The Research Report

Luke continued, "To get a better understanding of the changes we needed to make, I got the approval of the president of our company to head up a task force to find out how shifts in the environmental, technological, and demographic areas had impacted the selling process. Basically, we needed to find out what changes we needed to make in our sales strategy to make ourselves a more attractive vendor.

"We figured there was probably a fair amount of information out there to help us find out what we wanted to learn, but we really didn't know how to go about discovering and accessing it. So, we partnered with a couple of marketing professors who had been in my MBA program and had the experience and access to information on the changes and trends that were occurring in B2B buying behavior. They provided us with a comprehensive report which was distributed to our task force, and they also gave us a very informative presentation on the findings."

"So, what were some of the main conclusions of the report?" Paul inquired.

"Let me tell you the first key conclusion," Luke said with a smile. "As they finished their presentation they asked for our thoughts. I told them I was surprised to find out the way companies go through their buying process is really a lot different than we think it is."

"So how was that a main conclusion?"

"Right then one of the professors stopped, looked me straight in the eye and said, 'I've studied, worked with, and consulted with a lot of companies over the course of my career. One thing that I can tell you with the utmost certainty is that the two most dangerous words that are used in formulating a marketing strategy are *We Think*. Those two words have resulted in more negative outcomes for companies than I can count. Ladies and gentlemen, it doesn't matter what *We Think. It only matters what They Think.* You must understand how the customer thinks if you want to be successful.'

The two most dangerous words that are used in formulating a marketing strategy are We Think. It only matters what They Think.

"It was like a spotlight went on in my head," Luke continued. "Right then and there I realized that our entire sales approach was based on the *We Think* mentality. In looking around the room there were a lot of shocked looks from our folks. That really got our attention, and then and there we all knew that we needed to revise our entire sales process."

Luke continued, "We all decided to take a few days to study and digest the report. We then went on an off-site retreat for a couple of days to determine how to proceed. Based on the information from their report, we prepared our own report that gave us a roadmap. The results from that report and subsequent conversations with some of our customers, which I'll talk about in a little bit, resulted in this Pillar coming into being."

"And what were your conclusions?" Paul asked.

"I'm embarrassed to say as a company we discovered that we simply did not have a good handle on the key factors that were impacting how our customers were proceeding through their purchase journey to purchase our products," Luke said with a sheepish grin. "We realized that we needed to radically change the way we worked with our customers on that journey and had to do so in a hurry."

Luke walked over to his desk and picked something up.

"I can't give you our entire report as it contains some propriety information. However, I can provide you an executive summary which gives you the main findings," he said, handing Paul the summary. "There's a QR code on back cover which gives you the summary that should help you as you put notes in your notebook," Luke said. "Shall we get started by talking about what we found?"

Conclusions of the Report

Luke opened his copy of the summary and began to flip through it. "The overall theme of the report to our company was that the B2B purchase journey has become much more complicated, and I'll get to why we call it a journey in just a few minutes. As you've learned in other TBS interviews, the purchase journey has more people involved, encompasses more information, takes more time, and is simply more complex than just a few years ago. What was surprising to us was that all these changes have made it just as difficult for our customers to navigate their way through their purchase journey as it has for us to sell to them. As Serving Salespeople, we now must have a very good understanding of the struggles our customers are going through in their purchase journey. If we were going to transform our relationship with them and work to change their perspective, we needed to understand those struggles if were were going to guide them through their own transformation."

Paul jumped in. "I must say that I hadn't really considered how difficult the purchase process, er journey, has become for our customers," he admitted.

"Neither had we," Luke said. "Their report found that over three-fourths of B2B buyers agreed that the purchase journey has become much more complex and much more difficult. The report also told us that most salespeople are simply not grasping how complex the customers' purchase journey has become and still approach the process using an outdated sales framework. This really hit home with me because that was the exact reason I lost that sale."

Luke continued, "The report also pointed out that for many B2B customers the purchase journey has reached a 'tipping point,' where it is very difficult for the buying group to navigate through that journey without some, and in some cases a significant amount of, help from their vendors. They are constantly seeking more and better information from those vendors."

For many B2B customers the purchase journey difficult has become very difficult to navigate without some help from their vendors.

"As we were reviewing the research report, I was also part of the team developing the Seven Pillars of a Serving Salesperson. When our discussions turned to how we could better facilitate the purchase journey, I realized this concept naturally built on the learning from the first five Pillars. We refined our approach internally, and that work ultimately became the foundation for the Sixth Pillar. We realized that by facilitating our customers' purchase journey we would have an opportunity to begin to transform their perspective from thinking about their problems to considering their possibilities. As you've probably heard in your other interviews, the transforming process begins with the Serving Salesperson working with the customer to discover what some of those possibilities might look like. Rather than having them simply look at purchasing the product as a task to be competed, we saw the opportunity to transform our customers' thinking by helping them to clearly define their aspirations, question what they saw as limiting assumptions, imagine new possibilities, and then gain the confidence and clarity to move forward. I'll mention these points here, and when you talk to John Philips next month, he'll go into much more specifics on how you make that actually happen.

"However, there's also much more to facilitating the purchase journey than just sending their customers mountains of information that they can't or won't sift through. Many vendors also make it too difficult for their customers to find the information they are seeking on their websites. It became very clear to us that we as salespeople must work to make it easier for them to purchase our products."

Luke turned to the next page of the summary, and Paul could see bullet points in boldface type. "After a lot of discussion back and forth, we came up with four bullet points that we needed to engage in to facilitate the journey for our customers."

Paul had a thoughtful look on his face and then said, "So, how do we get ourselves out of the 'We Think' mentality and make sure we're on the right track?"

"To make sure we were on the right track, we provided the bullet points we came up with to facilitate the journey to some of our best customers to find out what *'They Think.'* We conducted a few video interviews both before and during our retreat to get our customers' feedback. As is always the case when you talk to your customers, those we talked to were very forthcoming and provided some very good recommendations. We revised our list accordingly and here's what we came up with," Luke said, pulling the summary report back out and showing Paul the next page.

Facilitate the Journey

- **Understand customers' buying journey**
- **Communicate on their terms**
- **Gather and summarize educational content**
- **Provide tools to enable the decision**

Understand Your Customers' Buying Journey

"In their presentation," Luke continued, "the professors stated that they decided on the term *buying journey* because *buying process* implies a more orderly, structured path to purchasing. For most of our careers all of us had assumed the process went linearly through a defined set of stages in a somewhat orderly fashion—recognize the problem, search for vendors, evaluate the vendors, and so forth. It was then our job to deal with the customers' needs at each stage of the process."

"Just how does the purchase journey differ from the purchase process?" Paul asked.

"Rather than progressing through discrete stages, now the buying journey consists of more fluid *tasks* that need to be completed," Luke said. "Oftentimes during the purchase journey the buying group will receive some new information which will necessitate them having to retrace their steps and reframe a purchase task they thought they had already completed. The purchase journey now has many more twists and turns and, as we just said, may even go back to a previous task if more information is needed or more work needs to be done. We therefore changed our sales approach from understanding the stages of the purchase process to identifying the different tasks the buying groups needed to complete, and then working together with them to help them complete those tasks."

"A number of times," Paul added, "I've seen my customers cycle back to a part of the purchase journey I thought we had already completed. I now can see that they were just going back to reevaluate a task."

Luke nodded in agreement. "Taking all this information into account gave us a much better perspective on our customers' purchase journey, and we revised our sales approach accordingly to integrate that information. Now when we begin a relationship with a customer, we first take the steps to understand the tasks that comprise their purchase journey. Understanding that journey has helped us become more successful."

Communicate on Their Terms

Luke turned to another page in the report. "Now, let's talk about the next point, which is how to communicate on your customers' terms. There were several things about how B2B customers gather and process information which opened our eyes to the different methods we need to employ to communicate with them. I know you've heard some of this information in your other interviews, so let me summarize.

"The report cited some research statistics on how modern buyers are accustomed to purchasing products for themselves online, and the same preferences they have for online personal purchases have extended into their B2B purchase behavior. They want things like instant access to information, a variety of options, fast delivery, and hassle-free returns. As you've also heard, the research showed that an increasing number of these younger demographics stated they would like to conduct most of the B2B purchase process online, with some even stating they did not want to interact with a salesperson at all. We'll address that a bit later."

"Marcos Simón and I talked about this, but this concerns me. I'd like to understand more," said Paul.

"We will," said Luke. "It sounds worse than it really is. But back to our point. We know that most B2B customers will conduct a *lot* of research online before even reaching out to a salesperson. We saw reports that show they are usually fairly far along in their purchase journey and usually will consult seven or more sources before even contacting a salesperson. They will reach out to such sources as current customers, personal referrals, company or product reviews, the company website, a competitor's website, industry associations, social media, and a general online search. This points back to the importance of an omnichannel marketing program that Marcos mentioned. We as marketers need to employ all channels of communication in our marketing efforts to ensure that the customers can access the information from a source of their choosing. Again, we must communicate on their terms.

"However," Luke continued, "even though customers are now more informed than ever, it doesn't mean they don't experience difficulties during the process. The report cited a research study that found that 89 percent of B2B buyers find buying online more complicated than in person, 66 percent are dissatisfied with their online purchase experience, and almost 50 percent experience problems often or always when purchasing a product totally online."

Paul looked confused. "I've heard a few times now that many customers said they prefer limited and maybe even no contact with their vendors," he said. "Yet they appear to be experiencing difficulties and dissatisfaction when they make purchases online. So how do we help resolve those issues?"

"I told you we'd get to that," said Luke with a wink. "It's a combination of old behaviors and new preferences. Even though B2B customers *say* they want to conduct their purchases with little to no contact with a salesperson, their behavior indicates otherwise. Remember that research has found that B2B customers will engage with their salesperson or vendor company an average of between five to seven times during the purchase journey. However, those communications that involve actual personal contact are becoming less frequent. A customer may occasionally want to see you or talk to you, but increasingly they will send you an email, text, instant message, or some other electronic form of communication asking for assistance or information. And as you've undoubtedly heard, they expect a response almost immediately. What we learned in our customer interviews is that there is an opportunity here to transform the relationship with our customers. Oftentimes there are a number of messages that go back and forth in a short period of time. Customers usually want to make a decision quickly, and providing them with the information they need when they need it can shift their perspective to preferring our products."

"This is interesting," Paul said. "Even though we're hearing a lot about how our customers want to minimize contact with salespeople, it's becoming evident that we need to be there for them."

"You're right," Luke responded. "One of the main conclusions of the report was that the majority of B2B buyers will need some sort of guidance through their purchase journey. I know that Lydia James mentioned that B2B buyers are exhibiting more risk aversion during their purchase journey. Research has shown that the number of interactions between customers and vendors has shown a dramatic increase in the past few years as customers are conducting their due diligence to reduce their perceived risk.

"Now, there's more to communicating on their terms," Luke said. "When customers log onto our websites or contact a salesperson, they expect to be able to gain the information they are seeking quickly and efficiently without having to jump through a bunch of hoops. Some feedback we heard in several of our interviews with our customers was along the lines of 'Don't just send me a bunch of links to articles and expect me to read them. Make it easy for me to find the information I need.'"

"Yikes!" Paul interjected. "We ask for a lot of customer information on our website before we provide *any* product information. Should we rethink this?"

"Yes, and a lot of companies need to," Luke said. "When a customer is asked for too much information, they will simply go to another website where they can access the information they are seeking more quickly and efficiently. And as I've already mentioned, when they do contact a sales representative, they expect the representative to answer questions in the moment in an informative, concise, and helpful manner.

"And one more thing, Paul. These modern customers expect to be treated as partners—but on their terms. Collaborating with the customer here not only transforms your relationship with them, but helps set the stage for guiding them through their own transformation which John Philips will talk about. We all know that companies need to have an omnichannel marketing strategy, so early in our communications with them we need to understand the information our customers are looking for. B2B customers expect to have access to a broader range of relevant information including pricing, business practices and policies, channel options, market feedback, and ongoing reports of customer experience and results. And they want all this to be available online. Like it or not, the customer is in control. We must be aware of what their expectations are and work to meet them in the best way we can without giving away the store." Luke stopped and sat back in his chair. "This is a lot to take in at one sitting. Why don't we take a break and go get a cup of coffee?"

"Your timing is good," Paul said. "I need a few minutes to let all of this sink in."

Luke and Paul took a quick walk to the coffee shop next door and returned to continue their conversation.

Gather and Summarize Educational Content

"The next section of the report is how to gather and summarize your educational content," Luke said, turning to the next section of the report. "The report concluded that we need to focus on *educating* our customers rather than simply providing them information," Luke said. "It found that customers want salespeople to educate them. That's why we used the term *educational content* rather than *product information*.

"Only providing product information is the 'We Think' mentality," said Luke. "We discovered that providing educational content is very different. Customers can find all the product information they need, and more, online. What we need to do is to expand upon that product information and provide them access to the type of additional resources that Marcos Simón mentioned—resources that can help them better understand how our products and services will benefit them. These are things like industry reports, reviews, articles, customer testimonials, and even instructional videos. It's about assisting our customers to make informed decisions and empowering them to get the most out of the products they buy from us. It's also about applying both our individual and our company's expertise to help our customers to work their way through their buying journey and reach a successful conclusion."

Provide your customers with the resources that can help them better understand how your products and services will benefit them.

Luke paused for a moment to make his point. "However, while we're making all this information available, it's important to remember that customers feel inundated with too much information. The research found that salespeople simply need to become better educators. A significant portion of B2B customers stated that they would find it very beneficial if vendors provided some assistance in putting together the information that's applicable to their purchase situation. The report referenced a study that found that a whopping 97 percent of B2B customers said it would be somewhat or very helpful to have all their buying research and resources in one place."

"So, what's the path to becoming a better educator?" asked Paul.

"Good question," said Luke, "and one we discussed a lot in the video conferences with our customers. They told us that if we're really going to assume the role of an educator, we need to assume the role of being content curators."

"What does that mean, exactly?"

"Like a curator in a museum, we need to collect, summarize, and make sense of the vast amount of information that's available to assist the customer with the task they are facing," Luke said. "It's finding and organizing industry reports, white papers, articles, reviews, and so forth and then putting them in a summary format that our customers can access and digest easily. Our role needs to be one of educating the members of the buying group better on the options they have available to them to help them resolve whatever issues they are facing. Also, we need to have an abundance mentality, offering this information efficiently, generously, and without obligation.

"And one final thought here," said Luke. "For the modern B2B customer, it's becoming less about *what* they know and far more about how they *feel* about what they know. The amount of information they can access is not the problem. What we can do is to help them have more confidence in our products' performance by being that content curator. We just need to provide the information in a form and through a channel that most appeals to that customer."

Provide Enablement Tools

Luke flipped over to the next page in the summary and continued.

"And that brings us to our final step to facilitate the journey for our customers. We need to provide the tools to assist the customers in their decision," Luke said. "Remember that the vast majority of B2B customers stated they would like to have a central location for the information they are seeking. What we're working on at our company is creating a content library that includes all the internal and especially external information that can provide answers to the most common questions the buying groups will ask."

"That sounds like a lot of work," said Paul, "Does doing all this work really make a difference?"

"Yes, it will," said Luke. "Their report stated that B2B customers are *much* more responsive toward sales representatives when the content library includes such information as customer case studies, industry articles, industry research reports and white papers, product videos, and demonstrations. That's what we're putting in our library."

"But won't the customer just take this information we provide and then go and buy from one of our competitors?" Paul asked.

"That certainly is a possibility," Luke answered. "But let me tell you some numbers that the report included:

- 95 percent of B2B customers select a vendor that provided them with content to help them navigate through their buying tasks involved in their journey.
- 82 percent of B2B customers viewed at least five pieces of content from their chosen vendor.
- 68 percent of customers feel more positive about a brand after consuming content about it."

"That's pretty convincing," said Paul with a nod.

"Now, let's continue by talking about enablement tools," said Luke. "We know that with the large product assortments that are carried by an equally large number of B2B vendors, product searches can provide a massive set of results. B2B customers are often searching for a specific product and do not want to sift through all those results to find what they want. The report found that about one-third of B2B customers say that finding the correct product they are searching for quickly and efficiently is their most significant pain point when searching online. Also, about 35 percent of B2B customers abandoned their shopping cart prematurely because they couldn't find their desired product fast enough.

"We know that the entire B2B world is beginning to discover how artificial intelligence can impact the entire marketing space. Did Marcos Simón talk about how their company is weaving machine and personal information together?"

"Yes," said Paul. "I thought that was an innovative idea."

"Indeed, it is," said Luke, "and we as vendors need to think about how we can use AI to our advantage. Research shows that one of the primary benefits of AI-powered search engines is the ability to both optimize conversion and increase the average order. This can also help vendors learn more about what products customers are really desiring."

Luke paused, took a sip of coffee, and leaned back in his chair for a moment, thinking about what he wanted to say next.

"At our company we are learning more about how the power of artificial intelligence can do some of our work for us. We've found that we can ask AI to summarize content on a broad range of topics. However, we've also discovered that we still need to edit that content before distributing it. But in the end, having the computer do the work for you can really increase your productivity and still supply you with the raw information that you can boil down and provide for your customers."

"So, what type of online capabilities should we think about developing at Petra?" Paul asked.

Luke paused for a moment. "Well, the move of B2B customers toward self-service tools is making offering customer portals an integral part of the B2B digital buying experience. These portals empower customers by giving them access to such things as account information, order history and status, and invoice history 24/7. Customer portals can increase online sales by integrating after-sale products and services to create high-margin, cross-selling opportunities. These portals can also help to centralize both sales and after-sales information in one single channel while at the same time giving your brand the tools to create an intuitive customer journey."

"Whew!" said Paul. "Technology is really continuing to have an impact on the entire process, isn't it?"

"That it is," said Luke. "And one last tool the report mentioned. B2B marketers can also employ virtual or augmented reality to enhance the customer's buying experience. Presenting products virtually allows customers to interact with them in a more immersive and realistic way and assists them in making more informed decisions. Augmented reality applications enable B2B customers to see things like fully rotating 3-D renderings of a product and view all the internal components and parts. We can also provide click-and-move product markups that can illustrate how to use complex and mechanical products."

Luke closed this report and sat back in his chair, indicating he had said all he wanted to say.

"Well, you know what to do next, don't you Paul?" said Luke. "We have some exercises for you to do in the notebook as well as at the website accessible by the QR code on the back of the report. We want you to begin to work them into your daily activities to where they become an integral part of your sales approach."

"Thank you—I think," said Paul with a grin. "And thank you for providing me with a summary of your research report. Just in the short time we've been together the information contained in the report has been very eye-opening."

"You're very welcome," responded Luke. "I know you're getting a lot of information thrown at you, but in the long run you'll see a benefit. I'll see you toward the end of the month, and I look forward to hearing some stories of how you have been able to facilitate the journey."

As was the case immediately after interviewing all the other members of the TBS, Paul left Luke's office with his head spinning from everything he had just learned. While he had certainly taken in a lot of information, he was wondering when he would have the chance to facilitate the journey for one of his customers.

It didn't take long for Paul to have the opportunity to put what he had learned from Luke into practice.

An Opportunity to Facilitate the Process

As Paul walked through the door of Mid-State Plastics a few days later, he could immediately could sense something was wrong. Pallets were backed up, operators were hovering, and Line Four—their highest volume conveyor— was sputtering on and off. Alex Phelps, the foreman who had asked him to come, didn't attempt to hide his frustration.

"Throughput's down again," he said. "We're losing almost an hour a shift. I think the drive motors are undersized, and we're probably going to need to replace them."

Paul could tell Alex was overwhelmed, and he knew overwhelmed buyers don't make good decisions. He simply said, "Let's go look at the conveyor belt and tell me what you're seeing."

As they watched the line, Paul noticed the belt would hesitate every few minutes and then surge to catch up. After walking around both sides of the conveyor belt he noticed the same thing happened several times. He crouched down and checked the rollers. It looked like there was resistance on some of the rollers and a few were binding.

"Alex, when was the last time these rollers were inspected?"

Alex gave a frustrated sigh and said, "We replace them when they fail. But they're not the issue. The motors are."

"Do you have a force gauge so I can measure the roller resistance?" Paul asked. Alex went and got a gauge and handed it to Paul who then measured the roller resistance. Paul stood up. "Your motors are encountering more friction than they were designed for. Replacing them won't fix the root cause. The rollers are the real bottleneck."

Alex let out a sigh of relief. "So, we've been chasing the wrong problem?" he asked.

Paul nodded. "Let's go back to your office and let me map out some options to remedy this situation." he said.

Back in Alex's office Paul laid out his solution to resolve the problem. "I'm not sure you need to replace all the rollers, so let's do this in stages. First, let's do a pilot test and replace the rollers on the worst thirty feet of the line. Then we'll measure the throughput for twenty-four hours both before and after those rollers were replaced. When we see the results we can decide if there was enough improvement to warrant replacing the rest of the rollers. If not, then we can begin to explore other options."

Alex nodded slowly. "That sounds like a good plan. How do we get this started?"

"Let me go back and put a proposal together," said Paul. "I can come back when it works for you, and we can have a meeting with whoever else needs to be here and go over what's involved."

Alex pulled out his phone and made a quick call. "The sooner the better. Would 11:00 tomorrow work for you?"

"I'll be here," said Paul.

The next morning Paul gave a presentation to Alex, the VP of production, and the controller. He began by providing a short summary of the root cause of the issue and then had a simple diagram showing how the friction on the rollers was overloading the motors' ability to handle it. He also found a video that illustrated the exact situation Mid-State was going through and the best way to solve it. He then laid out a plan for installing the pilot rollers complete with downtime estimates and finished with a projected ROI for various improvements in throughput. Alex's group approved the plan, and Paul set about ordering the new rollers and getting the installation team scheduled.

Paul was there to oversee the installation of the pilot rollers the next Tuesday, and when he came back on Friday throughput was up 12 percent. The belt was running steadily, the operators were no longer having to watch over the line, and Alex and his team were happy. Jane Riley, the controller, told Paul, "We can go ahead and order the full set of rollers. With the increase in throughput we will recover those costs in just over a year."

Alex then told Paul, "Let's schedule them to be installed on Line Three next. Thank you so much for all you did," he said, shaking Paul's hand. "We just couldn't figure out what was causing the problem. You not only found the problem, but you made all the arrangements to get it fixed. We really appreciate all you've done for us."

"Happy to be of service," Paul replied.

Back with Luke

The end of the month found Paul back in Luke's conference room sipping a cup of coffee while Luke reviewed Paul's notes. "Interesting! Wow! Very good," Luke said as he studied Paul's responses to the exercises. As he finished, he looked up and said, "So, tell me the story about helping your customer, Paul."

Luke had a wide smile as Paul finished his story.

"So, what have your learned about facilitating the journey?"

"As is the case with the other interviews, Luke, I've learned a lot. Building on the foundation of the first five Pillars of being a Serving Salesperson, I've learned the value of letting your true north of serving the customer drive all your other activities. When we focus our efforts on helping our customers navigate through their buying journey and thinking about how we can shift their perspective, we truly can serve their needs and transform the relationship we have with them."

"Paul, you've truly grasped the concept not only of what it means not only to facilitate the journey, but also how this Pillar fits into being a Serving Salesperson. If you put all of this into practice, 'You will eat the fruit of your labor; blessings and prosperity will be yours,' as it says Psalms 128:2. Next month you'll be talking to John Philips about Pillar Six: Guide the Transformation. I think you'll find that John is an excellent person to talk about that Pillar and will help you to see how all these Pillars fit together.

"Well done!"

Guide the Transformation

"Transformation does not start with someone else changing you; transformation is an inner self reworking of what you are now to what you will be."

—Bryon Pulsifer

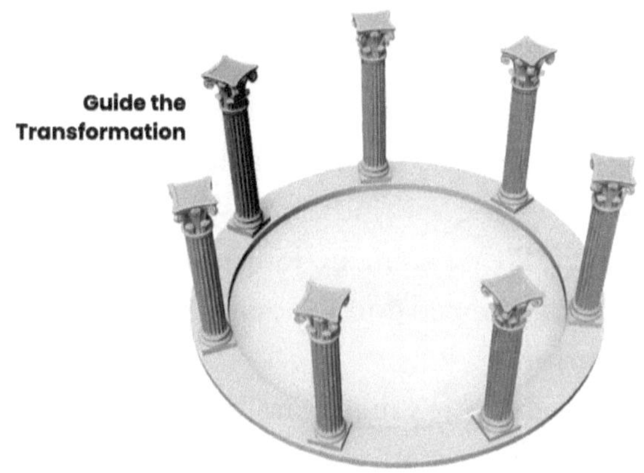

The Concept of Enough

THE FIRST TUESDAY in May was bright and sunny and Paul was on his way to his last meeting with the final member of the TBS on his journey toward becoming a Serving Salesperson. John Philips was a highly successful vice president of sales for a company that designed and produced machinery used to manufacture automotive parts. Like all the previous members of the TBS that Paul had met, John's reputation preceded him. Paul had come across an article in a local business journal that described how after John had led his firm to record sales each year for the past several years, he had changed directions and was now concentrating more on becoming a strategic resource for his clients.

That's where the article stopped, and Paul was anxious to learn more about his change in direction.

The meeting with John was a bit different than the others in that John had asked to meet with Paul at his home. He would soon learn why.

As Paul drove through the neighborhood to the address that John had given him, he felt more than a twinge of envy. As he came upon John's home he was immediately impressed as it was one of the nicer homes in the neighborhood with beautifully manicured landscaping and high curb appeal. Paul walked up the brick sidewalk and rang the doorbell, immediately hearing friendly barking.

An attractive woman who looked to be her mid-fifties opened the door and greeted him with a friendly smile. "Hello," she said, "You must be Paul. I'm Clarke Philips, John's wife, and this is Rosie," she said, motioning down to the beautiful golden retriever whose friendly demeanor and wagging tail indicated she was anxious to welcome Paul into her home. "Please come in. John's back in his office; he's been expecting you." Paul stopped for a moment to pet Rosie, who gladly accepted his attention.

"Hello, Paul. I see Rosie's made another friend." Paul looked up to see John, a man of medium stature and build with a beaming smile who also appeared to be in his mid-fifties. He was dressed casually in khakis, a polo shirt, and golf sweater. They shook hands and began to walk back toward John's office with Rosie following along.

"I'll bring you some coffee," Clarke called out behind them.

As they were walking John said, "I've been looking forward to meeting you. Let's go back to my office and get acquainted." They soon reached a bright spacious room at the back of the house. Windows ran the entire length of the back wall with a beautiful view of what John told him was the sixth hole of the private country club where John's home was located. At one end of the room was a sitting area around a large-screen TV. At the other end of the room was the area that served as John's home office. John sat in one of the conference chairs around a small circular table and motioned for Paul to sit in the other as Rosie curled up on her dog bed. "So, tell me, how has what you've learned changed your outlook on sales?" asked John.

Paul began to recount his story which he never tired of telling even though he had repeated it many times by now. He finished his story by saying, "Throughout my interviews there have been a number of mentions of how a Serving Salesperson should endeavor to transform the relationship with our customers and then guide them into transforming themselves. Everyone said that would all become clear when I talked to you."

"That leads us right into what I wanted to talk about," John replied. "It all started with one simple word."

"What word was that?"

"Enough."

"Enough?"

"Yes, enough."

"Now you've really got me intrigued. Tell me more."

"When I was younger and working to make a name for myself in the industry, like a lot of other hard-driving salespeople I set some lofty goals for myself and spent a lot of time chasing those goals. For a long time, I thought if I could get that next sale, make more money, or get one more promotion, then I would have enough. And you know what? When I got there, I discovered that enough wasn't enough. There was a whole other set of goals, a whole other level of wants that went with it, and I found myself constantly chasing after more and never having enough. Sound familiar, Paul?"

"All too," said Paul, thinking back to his previous priorities, "and what made you want to change?"

"It all changed dramatically one day about two years ago when of all things I was watching television."

"How did watching television make you want to change?"

"I was a candidate for president at another company. Not only would I be the president and get a significant pay increase, but I would also be given some equity in the company with the option to purchase more. Shortly after several interviews with both the owners and their board of directors I was in the grill room here at the country club when one of my friends came up to me and told me he had heard through the grapevine that I was a shoo-in for the job.

"I was so sure that I was going to get the job I began to make plans for the transition. I decided we could build that new, bigger house I'd always wanted on a vacant lot overlooking the twelfth green. I had even started negotiations to buy that lot."

John paused for a moment, and Paul was pretty sure he knew what was coming next.

"Then I got the 'we've decided to go in another direction' phone call. First, I was stunned. Then I was confused. Then I got angry. Really angry. I was so mad, disappointed, and upset that I didn't want to talk to anybody, didn't want to do anything. I knew no one was home, so I came home and threw myself down in front of the TV, too upset to do anything else. I was surfing through the channels and found a talk show discussing how people can turn negative feelings into positive ones. I thought, 'Boy, that's for me' so I stopped to watch.

"One of the guests was a psychologist who was discussing a sure and simple way to turn negative thinking into positive thinking: *do something for someone else.* He was saying that there is no better way to get your mind off your own problems than to focus your attention on meeting the needs of those around you. It's difficult to feel bitterness and depression when you're thinking about another person's needs and happiness. He went on to say that instead of looking for ways to make ourselves feel better, we should look for ways to make others feel better. When we think of the welfare of others, we can lift ourselves out of our own negative feelings and start thinking about the blessings and abundance that are available to us."

John hesitated for a minute. "Did Phoebe Andrews talk about some of the hormones that are released in emotional situations?" he asked.

"Yes, and it was fascinating."

"Well, the psychologist said similar things. He said that studies have shown that serving others can decrease cortisol, the stress hormone, while increasing oxytocin, which is related to positive social interactions and generosity. He also said that serving others can lower stress levels and promote feelings of happiness, calm, inspiration, and generosity. All these factors improve mental well-being and reduce depression and anxiety.

"The psychologist ended by telling us we all need to ask ourselves, 'Do I have enough? Do I really need any more? When you're feeling stress, depression, or anxiety, try turning your focus away from yourself to serving someone else who needs help.'"

A Realization

John paused for moment then continued. "The word *enough* really hit me like a ton of bricks. Then I thought about what the psychologist said and thought to myself, *Don't I have enough? Do I really need to have more?* Philippians 4:11 immediately came into my mind: 'for I have learned to be content whatever the circumstances.'"

"Then I looked around at our big house and all the possessions we'd accumulated. I also thought about our nice cars in the garage, our bank accounts, our investment and retirement portfolios—all the things I'd been pursuing to have 'enough.' That's why I asked you to come here today, to illustrate my point. Don't I look like I have enough? Did I really need a bigger house with more stuff?

"Then I began to think of the feeling of satisfaction I'd gotten when I had first transformed the relationship with my customers and then was able to shift their perspective and guide them through their own transformation in their operation that helped them achieve their desired objective. I remembered the joy I felt just a few weeks earlier when I'd gone to check on the progress of some machines that I had designed and my company had made for a small manufacturing plant that had been on the ropes. I had worked with my banker to help them secure a loan to buy our equipment. I helped to design the machines and worked with them to facilitate their buying journey. I then spent almost two weeks helping them install, calibrate, and get the equipment up and running. When I went back three months later the owner took me through the plant and showed me the production line where our machines were humming along very efficiently and effectively. I looked around and saw workers operating the machines who just a few months before didn't know if they'd still have a job.

"The owner shook my hand and thanked me for helping them secure the new machines. He told me they were able to provide cutting-edge products that gave them a competitive advantage. Also, he thanked me for the environmentally friendly design that fit with their sustainability initiative. They had been able to get enough manufacturing orders not only to get in the clear but to be in the black for a long time.

"As I sat in my car the thought hit me: I was not only able guide them through a transformation that improved their operation but also the situation for many of their relevant stakeholders. The equipment that I had designed and helped install allowed them to manufacture a state-of-the-art product that gave them a competitive advantage. Their employees had the security of knowing they would have a stable job well into the future. Their customers' customers were going to have a product that met their needs and allowed them to do their business better. With the environmentally friendly manufacturing process and a sustainable packaging design, society would benefit. Finally, what our company learned from designing those machines gave us some expertise that we could use for our other customers.

"I resolved then and there that I was going to expand my role from not only serving my customers but also to be a strategic resource, first by focusing on transforming my relationship with them. I would then seek to elevate their thinking from problems to possibilities, and then work with them to guide them through their own transformation so they could pursue those possibilities with confidence. I mentioned all this to Lew one day when we were playing golf, and the next thing I knew we were formulating this final Pillar."

For Paul that one word—*enough*—stuck in his mind and at the same time gave him a deep sense of remorse. He realized that he and Mary truly had had enough, yet he wanted more, really for no other reason than just to have it. He could only speculate on how his life might be different now if he had realized that simple concept long before this.

"Now," John said, "let's turn to the final Pillar: Guide the Transformation. By the time you've put the first six Pillars into practice with a customer, the relationship has typically deepened and started to evolve. And when the relationship changes, trust grows—and trust opens the door to greater possibilities.

"Paul, most customers want you to do more than simply solve their problem. They want someone who can help them see beyond the fix— to glimpse wider options, to imagine possibilities beyond the immediate solution, to consider opportunities that could reshape their future.

In short, many of them are ready to transform their thinking—and, in time, their entire operation. So now, let's assume you're ready to conclude the sales phase and invite them to move forward."

Well," said Paul, settling back into his chair, "I assume we're going to start by talking about closing the sale?"

"We're not going to talk about closing the sale," said John with a smile. "Closing the sale too often means pinning the customer down to make a purchase decision which often is a short-term fix and may or may not be the best for the customer in the long term. As a Serving Salesperson seeking first to transform the the relationship with the customer and then to elevate their perspective from problems to possibilities, I'll talk about how we work with them to first discover their ideal solution and then collaborate with them to determine the best way to achieve that solution. So, what we're going to talk about is what Phoebe Andrews talked about in *obtaining a commitment to advance the sale forward* and how that fits into the transformation process. Paul, according to research, how many B2B sales calls would you guess end up with either a definitive yes or no?"

"Well, based on my personal experience, I'd say less than half."

"It's actually lower—usually in the 20 to 30 percent range. Now, what do you have to obtain from the customer in order to move the sale forward?"

Paul thought for a moment and then said, "You have to get them to agree to make some sort of commitment to move forward."

"That's it," said John with a touch of pride in his voice. "To advance the sale means to obtain a commitment to advance to the next task in their purchase journey. Research shows that about two-thirds of salespeople do not ask for some type of commitment. However, if you do obtain a commitment, that same research says that the probability of the customer making a purchase rises dramatically—often reaching 70 percent or above."

"Now," said John, "there are always some sales calls where early on you realize there's not a fit either for your customer or you. For a Serving Salesperson, *no* is your second-most favorite answer. If there's not a fit between what you're presenting to them and their objective, it's best to recognize it right away and move on. However, in those sales calls where there is a potential fit between you and your customer, your key objective is to obtain a commitment to advance the sale forward. The best way to do that is to secure several smaller commitments before you ask for a larger commitment. And what do you use to get those smaller commitments?"

"Trial closes?" Paul said hesitantly.

"You're right. Define a trial close for me."

"I think of a trial close as getting your customer to decide on a minor point like choosing the standard or deluxe model or having the product installed or installing it themself."

"That's correct, Paul. And why do you think psychologists tell us that it's important to gain commitments, especially an initial commitment, from your customer?"

"To get them used to saying yes?"

"That's partially correct," John replied. "But a more important reason is that psychologists have found that when individuals are faced with making a series of decisions, the first couple of decisions they make become an anchor for their later decisions. This is due to what psychologists call *behavioral consistency*. Individuals tend to make decisions that are consistent with their previous decisions. Studies have shown that getting a person to agree on one issue will boost the likelihood of getting their agreement on another issue by about 60 percent."

> ## Behavioral Consistency
>
> **Individuals tend to make decisions that are consistent with their previous decisions.**

John sipped his coffee and continued. "Now, when you want to ask for a commitment to move the sale forward, there's a significant caveat to take into account."

"Such as?"

"Think back to what Luke Matthias talked about in Understanding your Customer's Buying Journey. When deciding what commitment you're going to ask for, you need to understand where the customer is on their buying journey and what their next purchase task will be. You cannot ask for a commitment greater than the customer is able to give you at that point in their journey. It is best to only ask for a commitment that will help them advance to the next purchase task on that journey. If it leads to a commitment to purchase, so much the better. However, it can become risky to ask for a commitment greater than they're able to give you at that point in their buying journey.

"Now, let's fast-forward to the point where you're going ask them to make a commitment to advance the sale forward. There are a number of ways to ask your customer to make that commitment, and we coach our salespeople to use an approach that they are comfortable with and fits the situation. Here are some possible approaches we give to our salespeople," said John, pulling out a sheet of paper.

- Propose a commitment.
- Make a direct request.
- Summarize all the decisions they made with their trial closes.
- Present a balance sheet.
- Give them pros and cons.

"And one final thing," said John. "When you do receive an order, either in person or virtually, make sure that you get all the information right then that you need to process their order. It's embarrassing and makes you look incompetent when you need to contact them to obtain some clarifying information."

John continued, "Paul, a Serving Salesperson not only seeks to transform the relationship with their customers but also to transform their thinking in how they perceive their situation, to help them to recognize a different perspective, and gain a clarity they didn't have before. When we can fundamentally shift our customers' perspective from where they are to where they want to be and guide them through transforming their own operations that allow them to be more productive and profitable, we are truly serving our customers in a way very few other salespeople do.

"However, before we even start guiding the customer's transformation, there's a very important point to keep in mind. Matthew Solomon talked about having an internal compass that always points to your own personal true north of serving the customer. That always needs to be top of mind. As a Serving Salesperson, we always seek to serve the customer to the best of our ability. We don't push transformation; we strive to create the conditions necessary to guide the customer into transforming themselves. By implementing the principles of the Seven Pillars throughout their purchase journey, we have shown the customer that we have their best interest in mind and can lead them through their transformation. As you learned from Phoebe Andrews, you need to have earned prestige by implementing the principles of the Pillars of a Serving Salesperson. You must have built that deep, trusting relationship that Marcos Simón talked about that makes the customer *willing* to be transformed. It's not about being liked, impressive, or persuasive. It's about becoming the consummate Serving Salesperson that a customer trusts to guide their transformation.

"A transformation of a customer's operation can run the whole gamut. It can be as simple as showing them what keys to push on their keyboard to make a software program easier to use all the way to overseeing a complete overhaul of one of their business operations. It's not the extent of the transformation that's important; it's the impact it has. Martha Peters talked about having a passion for serving our customers. Whatever transformation is called for, as Serving Salespeople we can call upon that passion to guide our customers into elevating their thinking, to change their perspective, to see the situation they're facing in an entirely different way, and to aspire to achieve something bigger and more beneficial to all their relevant stakeholders."

John paused for a minute to take sip of coffee. "I've already mentioned some examples and measures you learned in your interviews that you can use to begin to transform your customers' thinking. As we discuss the process of guiding the customer into transforming themselves, I'm going to refer to those conversations you had with the TBS members. By the time we've finished you hopefully will have a clear picture of how we bring the key principles of the Seven Pillars together and discuss how we can truly guide that transformation for our customers. So, shall we begin our discussion on how to guide the transformation?"

"I'm all ears," replied Paul.

Transforming Their Perspective – Discovery

"Before we get started, what did both Lew and Matthew tell you was necessary for you to adopt the mindset of being a Serving Salesperson?"

"They told me I had to be transformed by the renewing of my mind."

"So, just as your mind has been transformed, you now need to work to transform the minds of your customers. By transforming your mindset and embracing the principles of the Seven Pillars of a Serving Salesperson, you've already begun to transform the relationship with your customers. That transformed relationship now allows you to guide your customers into elevating their perspective, to change their mindset from problems to possibilities, and to help them visualize what success for them could look like.

> *Guiding customers into discovering the solution on their own is an effective tool towards transforming their thinking and changing their behavior.*

"There are three phases to transforming your customers' perspective: discovery, collaboration, and integration," said John. "Let's begin by talking about discovery—helping our customers discover what possibilities might exist for them. It's very important to guide our customers into *discovering* the solution on their own. Neuroscientists are convinced that the insights individuals gain on their own is an effective tool to guide them toward transforming their thinking and therefore changing their behavior.

"Let's go back to when Phoebe Andrews told you about asking the WIMITY question. Let's assume you have received the answer to the WIMITY question and have started to peel the onion. Once you understand the factors that are most important to the customer, you can begin the customer's discovery process by changing the focus of your questions from *problem-centered questions* to *solution-centered questions*. Solution-centered questions encourage your customers to expand their thinking and project out into the future and articulate what an ideal solution might look like for them. You can build on the information you learned from the WIMITY question and use it to expand the discovery process.

> ### *The three phases to transforming your customer's perspective*
>
> **Discovery**
>
> **Collaboration**
>
> **Integration**

"The discovery phase is where you begin to transform the customer's thinking by shifting their perspective of their situation. Combine the passion for serving that you learned from Martha Peters with the sharpened EQ you learned from Lydia James to get them to stop thinking about their problems and ask solution-centered questions that guide them toward expanding their possibilities. Help them visualize a clear picture of what their ideal solution would look like. Ask questions like 'What outcome would feel like a win for you?', or 'What would excellent look like instead of just acceptable?' Then, as you did before, peel the onion. When they give you an answer to your first question, you can peel the onion further by simply asking questions like, 'What would be the value of that?' or 'How would that help?" Your customer is almost always going to know more about the benefits to them than you are, so guide them into discovering those benefits as possibilities for themselves. Record this information as you'll be using it again when it comes time for the integration process.

"Once we've gotten the customer to articulate their desired outcome," continued John, "help them realize that the barriers they think they have are *not* insurmountable. You'll probably need to quietly point out that it's likely they're going to have to change their current approach to viewing their issues. Ask questions like 'What assumptions are you making about this process that might no longer be true?' or 'What's the cost of staying where you are?' Have them list the obstacles and sort them into such groups as symptoms, root causes, constraints, and assumptions."

John continued, "It's important to understand that a transformation will not come about unless the customer *believes* it can be achieved. To overcome the doubts they may have, think about what Phoebe Andrews told you about brain-friendly communication. At this point the negative neural networks the customer has are probably going to kick in, so you need to focus on the positive outcomes of the transformation. Once the customer sees the gap between where they are and where they want to be, begin to expand their sense of possibilities. Get them to think about how they have seen a transformation occur in their own company or one they are familiar with. Share stories of similar transformations and use those to facilitate a discussion around potential scenarios. Ask them, 'If nothing was holding you back, what would you try first?' or 'What would it look like if you eliminated this bottleneck entirely?' "

It's important to understand that a transformation will not come about unless the customer believes it can be achieved

---

"Confidence is not something the salesperson gives. It's another thing the customer needs to discover on their own. Shift the customer's thinking from hope to ownership. Focus on determining the strengths and resources the customer has and show how they can employ those strengths and resources to achieve their desired goal. Ask things like 'What strengths do you have that will help you succeed?' or 'What's one step that you could take immediately that would move you forward?' Make them feel that their stated goal is achievable. Once you have gotten them through to discovery and they want to move toward their desired goal, that is the time to ask for their commitment to advance the sale forward to that next step."

John paused for a moment and asked, "How are we doing so far?"

"Very thought provoking. Let's keep going."

Collaboration

Straightening up in his chair, John continued, "If you have transformed the relationship with your customer in all likelihood you have collaborated with them. Once you have gotten your customer to elevate their thinking and give you a commitment to advance the sale forward, our next step is to endeavor to create a *culture of collaboration*. A culture of collaboration is where we work together with our customers to move them beyond simply solving their problem toward achieving the aspirational goal they have visualized. Together we collaborate to shift their thinking, to guide them into thinking bigger, more creatively, and more aggressively.

"Now, I have a question for you," said John. "What would be the value of having the customer discover a solution on their own and then collaborating with them to determine a path forward?"

"If they thought of it, I would think they'd be much more willing to consider it as their own idea."

"That's exactly right. When the customer sees their own perspectives being factored into the solution, it allows them to take *psychological ownership* of that solution. Customers who take psychological ownership feel that the main reason to move forward is to achieve their own perspective, not the salesperson's. They will have a greater sense of control, a greater depth of knowledge of the agreement, and a greater sense of self-investment because they feel the solution is theirs. One study asked corporate decision-makers to list the qualities that top salespeople exhibited. Of the forty qualities evaluated, "collaborated with me" was the number two factor after "educated me." When a salesperson collaborated with their customers to find new ideas, 95 percent of those customers stated this would make them more willing to collaborate with that salesperson again."

When the customer sees their own perspectives being factored into the solution, it allows them to take psychological ownership of that solution and move forward is to achieve their own perspective.

John paused for a moment before continuing. "At this point you want the customer to articulate the need for transformation themselves. Like you did in the discovery phase, you ask solution-centered questions that lead them to their own conclusions. Create the conditions where the customer names it, owns it, and desires it. Ask them questions such as 'If this worked exactly the way you hope it will, what would your team be able to accomplish?' or 'What decision here aligns most with the future you're trying to build?' You reflect their insights back to them and then summarize what they said in a way that clarifies the path going forward. Again, your sharpened EQ helps you understand the customer and their desires. They are not going to commit to a transformation based on logic alone. They're going to commit to it because it also appeals to their reactive system and aligns with who and what they want themselves and their company to become.

"Then," John continued, "bring in what you learned from Luke Matthias about how to facilitate the purchase journey. Build the new model together; make decisions collaboratively. In all likelihood this is new territory for your customer, so use your EQ to create psychological ownership and safety at every step. Tell them it's okay to not know the answer right now and keep affirming their courage to explore new territory. Always frame the customer as the hero. It's *their* insights and *their* discoveries. *They* are using *their* strengths to progress forward, and *they* are leading this change. Finally, maintain alignment with the goal they've set for themselves. The transformation has a much greater chance of success if it's positioned as a natural extension of who the customer wants to be."

"I have a question, John," said Paul. "I've had times, and I'll bet you have too, when you thought the customer you were working with was being sincere in their discussions during the process. However, when you were too far down the road to turn back, you discovered that they were in it for an 'I win you lose' outcome, and you end up getting taken advantage of. How can we avoid that?"

"A good point, Paul, and one all salespeople have faced," John replied. "First, if we're sincere in creating a culture of collaboration, even the most skeptical customers can come around and want to engage with you. However, we must be realistic and know that there are going to be some customers who are only concerned with what's in it for them."

"So how do we recognize people who are trying to take advantage of us and deal with them?"

"There are a few signs that people who are not sincere will give off," John said. "From the outset they usually are impatient, concerned only about their own interests. Next, they are often very defensive and not open to others' viewpoints. Also, insincere people are not consistent in their communication. Their words, actions, and beliefs will change over time. Finally, watch their body language. Sincere individuals typically display open and positive body language. They make good eye contact, have a relaxed posture, and use appropriate gestures. Insincere individuals tend to have lack of eye contact, tense or rigid posture and gestures, and inconsistent vocal tone and pitch. When you see an individual exhibiting some of these signs, you need to decide if it's worth continuing with that individual."

"So, what's the solution for when we realize that we're dealing with a customer who is trying to take advantage of us and we see our actions beginning to infringe on our own self-interest?" Paul asked.

"Good question," John answered. "In those situations the best strategy to avoid getting taken advantage of is to switch from being a devoted giver to being a matcher, engaging in a tit-for-tat strategy. As Serving Salespeople we start out with the posture of a devoted giver and stay cooperative until it's clear the customer has switched from cooperating to competing. When that happens, research has found that the best strategy is to be a matcher two-thirds of the time and a devoted giver one-third of the time. This can help you achieve a powerful balance of discouraging your customer from being a taker while still serving without being too punitive. This also gives the other party an opportunity to revert to a collaborative mode.

"However, while you are devoted to going above and beyond in serving your customer, sometimes you will reach a point where sacrificing your and your company's best interest can no longer be justified and it's untenable to continue. Even though we try not to, sometimes it's best to professionally agree to disagree and part company."

"Thanks," said Paul, "this is helpful."

"Now, how about taking a break for a few minutes before we finish up?" said John.

"Works for me," replied Paul, "I've got a lot swimming around in my head after that last section and could use a few minutes to let it settle in."

Paul and John spent a few minutes walking around John's backyard on the beautiful spring morning. Both agreed it was a perfect day for a round of golf. John invited Paul to play a round with him, and they decided to do so when Paul returned for his follow-up conversation at the end of the month.

Feeling a bit refreshed after their break and sipping a fresh cup of coffee, Paul and John returned to John's office to finish their conversation.

Integration

"Now let's move onto the integration stage—laying out just how this transformation is going to take place," John continued. "When the customer has elevated their thinking and you have collaborated to plan the transformation, that's when the Serving Salesperson shifts from salesperson to guide. When you've reached this point with your customers, they are going to be open, curious, and willing to explore options. As their guide in the process, you need to be their partner and provide them with the structure and momentum to help them understand how to move forward.

"Customers generally fear ambiguity more than change, so you need to make their transformation feel both safe and structured.

Remind them that they don't have to decide everything at once. Refer back to the ideas they had in the discovery phase when they imagined what their ideal situation would look like. Show that the transformation can be phased in and work with them to map out a structured plan for how it will happen. Once a customer is aligned with moving forward, you need to reiterate that they are in charge, and your role is to guide them through their own transformation journey. You can ask questions such as 'What matters most to you as you move through this change?' 'What's the next step that feels both realistic and meaningful?' and 'What challenges do you anticipate along the way and what's the best way to handle those challenges when they show up?'

"The whole process can fall apart if the customer feels overwhelmed. Build up their confidence and ability to carry out this transformation with statements such as 'Everything you've shared tells me you're more prepared for this journey than you realize' or 'The way you're thinking about this tells me you're absolutely capable of leading this shift.' Here's where you need to cycle back to their existing strengths and assets. Work with them to create a list of how they can employ these strengths and assets to move forward.

"You also need to normalize the challenge for them and make the path feel manageable. Reinforce the fact that this transformation is doable. Statements like 'Teams in your exact situation have completed this shift, and you're starting from a stronger place than most' and 'This doesn't require a leap, just a series of small, smart steps'.

"Work on helping them to illuminate a clear path forward. The customer has determined their desired outcome, seen the gap, and identified the possibilities. Now it's your job to translate that into a definitive plan. Reassure them with a statement such as 'We'll navigate this together,' 'You won't have to figure this out on your own,' and 'I'm here to help you make confident, informed decisions throughout the process.' Build out a 30, 90, and 180-day plan. Identify the key milestones and timelines. Clarify roles. Explain what the customer is going to do, what the salesperson will support, and what success will look like. Jointly compose a written document to guide the process. Writing things down will force you to think about the proposal and will provide a record of what you've agreed to and what the future activities will look like.

"Finally, reiterate to all the relevant parties that transformation is a process, not an event. The transformation is not going to happen in a single meeting. It's going to happen first in the customers' minds and then in the subsequent actions they take. Schedule short meetings every few weeks to get updates and to revisit goals and aspirations. Celebrate the small wins with them and reinforce their process with statements like, 'You're becoming the kind of manager who can...'"

John leaned back in his chair, indicating he was finished.

"So, Paul, what are your thoughts on how to guide the customer into transforming themselves?" John asked.

"Our discussion has really shown me how the Seven Pillars all fit together," said Paul. "Throughout all my interviews I've increasingly seen how the Pillars are intertwined and support the structure of being a Serving Salesperson. You have really given me a very clear picture of how the mindset of a Serving Salesperson works and shown me how the principles of the Seven Pillars come together to serve the customer as well as to allow us to first transform our relationship with them and then guide them into transforming their own operation. Thank you very much, John, for your insight."

"Oh, no thanks necessary, Paul. Our goal is to serve the customer the best way possible, and the Seven Pillars provide you a framework to do so.

"Well, you know the drill don't you, Paul?" John said with a smile. "Let's look at the exercises you'll be doing over the next few weeks."

Paul turned to the exercises based on what he and John had talked about—things like guiding the customer to discover their needs, collaborating with the customer, and mapping out how to integrate the transformation. Looking up, he said, "Well, it looks like I've got some work to do before we meet again."

"I've enjoyed our time together, Paul. Rosie and I will walk you out."

Back at the Office

As soon as Paul walked into the office, an administrative assistant called out to him.

"Gary said he wants to see you when you come in."

A whole series of thoughts immediately ran through Paul's mind. He walked right over to Gary's office and lightly tapped on the open door.

"Come in, Paul, and sit down," Gary said with a big smile on his face, relieving Paul's trepidation. "I understand you spent some time with John Philips this morning. How'd it go?"

Paul gave Gary an abbreviated version of the events and finished up rather quickly so they could get to the purpose of the meeting.

Gary sat back in his chair and took in and let out a deep breath.

"Paul, this morning I got an urgent phone call from a customer who's having a problem with one of the machines on their production line. I'd like you to be the one to go over there and see if you can help them."

Paul's heart leaped with the excitement that a salesperson always gets at the news of a potential customer.

"Of course I'll go see them! Who is it?"

"Walters Enterprises."

The excitement immediately turned to a queasy feeling in Paul's stomach.

After giving Paul a minute to let it sink in, Gary continued.

"Paul, I think both you and Petra are ready to put the past behind you and mend the fences. May I tell them you'll be contacting them?"

Paul sat there with his head down, his mind spinning with all kinds of thoughts for what seemed like an eternity. Finally, he slowly lifted his head and said softly, "Make the call."

At Walters Enterprises

Sitting in the lobby at Walters Enterprises later that afternoon, Paul was understandably nervous. He had had no contact with anyone at

Walters Enterprises since the capacitor order was canceled several months ago. Walters Enterprises had contacted Gary about a problem they were having with their laser cutting machines, and since Paul had a fair amount of experience dealing with those machines Gary decided to ask him to visit Walters. All sorts of thoughts were swirling around in Paul's head about what was going to happen next.

"Hi, Paul," a voice called out, jarring Paul from his thoughts. He looked up to see Griffin McDaniel, the production manager, standing before him.

"Hi, Griffin, it's good to see you again," said Paul, extending his hand, his voice trying to sound as confident as he could.

"Nice to see you again too," said Griffin, shaking Paul's hand. However, the strain in his voice showed that his attempt at politeness was clearly a stretch for him.

As they sat down in the conference room, Paul came right to the point. "Griffin, I want to thank you most sincerely for allowing Petra and me the privilege of coming to see you again. I can't tell you how sorry I am for the way I handled the situation with the capacitors last year, and I ask for your forgiveness. I have no excuses. I was wrong in the way I handled things, and I was wrong for not telling you the whole truth about the capacitors."

Paul noticed Griffin's suspicious look appeared to soften somewhat, so he continued. "I don't know if you'll believe this or not, but I've changed. I've been working with several salespeople who are true Serving Salespeople, and they've had a tremendous impact on me. I've totally changed my mindset and the way I approach sales, and now my focus is first to deepen my relationship with my customers and then to help them discover what possibilities might exist for them. I'm asking you to give me and Petra one more chance."

Griffin stared at Paul for what seemed like an eternity. Finally, he asked, "So, tell me, how does one become a Serving Salesperson?"

"Well, here's what I've learned. . . ."

Mother's Day

The next Sunday was Mother's Day, which Paul had been looking forward to with great anticipation. For the first time since they had separated, Mary had agreed to allow him to take her and the girls to church. Some time ago he had made reservations for a Mother's Day brunch at Mary's favorite restaurant.

After church in the parking lot Elizabeth spoke up. "Dad, we need to go home so I can get my cell phone," she said.

"Your cell phone? What for?"

"In case someone from my team for the class project calls or texts me."

"But Elizabeth, it's noon on Sunday. Who's going to call or text you now?"

"Please, Dad, I wouldn't want to miss something."

"Oh, all right, but please don't take too long. I don't want to be late for our reservation."

As they pulled into the driveway, Paul noticed that Nathan and Susan Brown and their children were standing in their driveway next door. As soon as Paul stopped the car, both girls threw their doors open and ran over to meet their neighbors.

"We're going to lunch with the Browns," Elizabeth called over her shoulder, "I guess you and Mom are going to have to go by yourselves."

Paul shot a quizzical look at Mary, who looked just as surprised as he did. "Did you know anything about this?" he asked her.

"No," she said, and then broke out into a shy smile. "But it looks like we have a date," she said, with her chin down and turning her head slightly toward him.

"Have a nice brunch, you two," Susan called out as she climbed into her car with all the kids in tow.

Paul looked over at Mary and smiled. "I guess we do have a date," he said. All of a sudden he was filled with the same nervous excitement he had felt early in their relationship when he was taking her someplace special. "Shall we go?"

"We shall," said Mary definitively, plopping both hands in her lap, smiling from ear to ear.

The brunch was all Paul could have hoped for, and more. Their table for two (Nathan knew the owner and had modified the reservation) was nice and private, the food was wonderful, and the service impeccable. As they talked, they enjoyed a stunning view of a beautiful flower garden bursting forth on the warm spring day. It was their first date together in well over two years, and it was clear to any observer that they were enjoying each other's company. After bringing Mary up to date on the progress of his interviews with members of the TBS, Paul stopped for a moment.

"Mary, what's one thing that you dream about, one thing you'd like to accomplish, one goal you'd like to meet?"

"One thing I dream about?"

"Yes, what do you really wish and hope for? I know you always wanted to get your CPA, but you put that aside when the girls were born. What do you wish for now?"

"I don't know. I guess I hadn't thought about it much for the past few years."

"I know you haven't, and that's my fault. You know one thing that all this learning about being a Serving Salesperson has made me realize? What a great servant you are, Mary, to the kids, to me, to your parents, to your friends, to everyone. You have always considered others before yourself, constantly putting your interests aside to meet the needs of others. When I think about what a true servant is, Mary, I think of you."

Mary cocked her head slightly as a surprised expression came over her face.

Paul continued, "All the pain and heartache I've caused you and our family, Mary, it's all my fault. I want to make it up to the girls, but I especially want to make it up to you. I realized that I was always chasing after something more and that I was never going to get there. I've come to realize that I—I mean we—really do have enough and that I need to quit chasing after more stuff. From now on I'm going to focus on being a servant to not only my customers but also to the girls, and especially to you. And I want to help you achieve your dreams, Mary, whatever they may be."

Mary's eyes were now glistening. "Thank you, Paul," she finally said in a halting voice, reaching over to squeeze his hand.

Back with John Philips

Just after the Memorial Day holiday Paul was back at John's house. As had become the pattern by now, Paul had given John his now well-worn journal, and John was reading through it, nodding approvingly at Paul's responses to his exercises and the notes he had taken.

"So, tell me what you've learned."

"The concept of *enough* is something that's really stuck with me, John. When I internalize the idea that I really do have enough, then I can be truly focused on serving my customers and working to transform my relationship with them and endeavor to shift their perspective to help them to become more productive and profitable."

"Excellent, Paul," said John. "That one word changed my way of thinking, and I hope it does the same for you.

"So how did it go at Walters Enterprises?"

"How did you know about that?" said Paul.

"Oh, let's just say a little bird told me."

"Well, when I got there, Griffin McDaniel, the production manager who I had the appointment with, was a bit cool at first. However, when I told him what I've been learning about being a Serving Salesperson over the past months and then turned the conversation to being there to serve them and help them solve their problem, he really opened up, and we had a great discussion.

"One of the products we supply for them is a lubricant called slide-way oil which is used to lubricate the rack and pinion tracks, guide rails, and bearing shafts on their high-tech Italian laser cutting machines. Griffin had called our VP of sales, Gary, because he had just discovered that the plant only had a two-day supply of slideway oil on hand and was also having a problem with the bearing shafts on one of their machines. Keeping the bearings properly lubricated is very important to keep the machine running smoothly.

"Griffin told me that they like to keep at least a fourteen-day supply of the slideway oil on hand, and he had discovered that they had only had enough to get them through the next day. It turns out that the woman who managed their inventory had had a very difficult pregnancy and was off work a lot for the two months before her baby was born. The baby was born prematurely a month ago, and she had decided to stay home with her full time. They had been limping along with their inventory control since she left. They had just hired a replacement, but that person wouldn't be starting for two more weeks and then they had the onboarding learning curve.

"I saw the fallout right after I walked into their storeroom. A quick scan around the room told me several of the items were outdated, and there were also some unopened boxes on the floor that clearly had not been entered into their system. Rather than simply ordering some more slideway oil for them, I sensed an opportunity to transform not only their ordering process for the oil, but how we might be able to transform a part of their business operation. My mind went back to our conservation about the three phases of transformation: discovery, collaboration, and integration. I told Griffin that I would get to work on ordering the oil and would find him when I needed him.

"I arranged to have a fourteen-day supply delivered that afternoon. Then I went through their storeroom and found some lubricants and machine parts that were no longer applicable for their machines. I separated out the inventory that they didn't need and in a few phone calls sold it to other manufacturers, which freed up some space and helped their cash flow.

"I then began the discovery phase of the transformation. I found Griffin and asked him the WIMITY question. What was the most important thing to him to resolve this situation? He told me they were having problems with getting the laser cutters lubricated properly and he wanted to fix that problem. I then peeled the onion and asked just what exactly did 'fix that problem' mean. He told me that they always seemed to be scrambling to have enough slideway oil on hand and that the employees were lubricating the laser cutting machines by hand and would often overlubricate the machines just to make sure there was no damage. That process was very labor intensive, and the over lubrication wasted an appreciable amount of expensive slideway oil. He also said that there was no one responsible for making sure the machines were lubricated regularly, and the reason they called us was because the bearing shafts on one of the machines had not been lubricated properly which had shut down that machine. He asked me for help fixing these issues.

"I then continued the discovery process with a solution-centered question. I asked him, 'What would an ideal outcome look like for you?' He said that it would be having a reliable supply of slideway oil and the machines working properly all the time with no hiccups. I then peeled the onion some more and discovered that having the machines working properly meant having an adequate supply of lubricants, knowing when to lubricate the machines, and making sure they were lubricated properly with the right amount of oil in a timely matter.

"I then asked another solution-centered question: 'What would be the benefit of having a system that would handle all of that for you?' He got a relieved look on his face and said, 'That would mean more productivity for our machines and a whole lot fewer headaches for me.' I said, 'How about you let me help you get there?', and he gave me a commitment to advance the sale forward.

"To begin the collaboration phase, I made an appointment for the next week with him, the VP's of production and engineering, and the chief financial officer to go over my recommendations. I was aware of some automatic lubricating systems for laser cutting machines, so when I got back to my office, I did some online research and discovered two vendors that offered systems that could fit Walters' machines that I could partner with to sell to them. Both companies had very complete product descriptions and instructional videos on their websites, so I set about gathering the information to present to Walters. I spent the next day learning about each of the lubricating systems the two companies offered and dug around and found a couple of industry reports and reviews of the two systems by experts in the industry. I prepared a summary of the two systems, complete with the product features, engineering specifications, labor and maintenance requirements, and a financial analysis of each system.

"The next week I went back and made a presentation to the buying group. I provided a written summary of the key points for their consideration as well as my analysis of each of the two systems. We finished by looking at the videos for both systems. When they asked me what system I thought was best, in the spirit of collaboration I turned the question around and asked them which system *they* thought would be best. We then had a group discussion about how they would see each system impacting their inventory costs, production efficiency, and financial performance. As they have four laser cutting machines, purchasing a system for all four machines would be a significant expense, so that entered the conversation. I had discovered that each system had been installed on laser cutting machines for local companies, so I arranged a visit for the team to view a product demonstration for each one.

"We met again after they had viewed those demonstrations, and I led one more discussion. I made a concerted attempt to get everyone's input, and as they were having the discussion, I observed that they were taking psychological ownership of the decision, valuing their own perspectives. It truly was a group decision. They decided to order one system as a trial on one machine, and if the results were as they hoped, they would add the system for their other machines.

"As long as I had everyone there, I began the integration phase of the transformation. I had analyzed their ordering of the slideway oil and recommended we automatically deliver a month's supply of oil on the first Monday of every month. The lubricating system would indicate when the oil reservoir needed to be filled, so I set up an appointment first to work with their IT team to make sure those notices were directed to the proper individuals and then with their maintenance team to show them how to properly refill the reservoirs. We then set up another meeting thirty days after the first system was installed to evaluate how the system was working. We decided that our agenda for that meeting would be to determine if they wanted to go ahead and put automatic lubricating systems on their other three machines and if so, what that schedule would look like. Finally, I contacted the manufacturer of the machine, and they sent out a technician that got the idle bearing shafts lubricated and working properly.

"After the meeting was over, Griffith McDaniel walked me out and thanked me very profusely, telling me not only had I solved the problem but had positively changed their operation and given him a whole lot less to worry about. What was a bothersome maintenance activity that they were always struggling with was taken care of and now they were able to focus their efforts more productively. Griffith felt pretty strongly that they would end up with the lubricating systems on all four machines, and he was already looking forward to that happening. With having a constant supply of slideway oil and the machines being properly lubricated, he was very optimistic that their productivity would noticeably increase and have a very positive impact on the company's profitability.

"Working with Walters Enterprises really served as a capstone experience for me," said Paul. "I was really able to see how the principles from the Seven Pillars came together to truly shift a customer's perspective from thinking about problems to possibilities, and to transform their operation into becoming more productive and profitable. I really feel that brought together all the principles of a Serving Salesperson for me."

John beamed. "That's truly what being a Serving Salesperson is all about, seeking to first transform the relationship with your customer and then to guide them to think past their problems to envisioning what's possible just as it says in Ephesians 4:23: 'to be made new in the attitude of your minds.' Paul, based on what I've heard and have now witnessed firsthand, it certainly appears to me that you have transformed yourself into becoming a Serving Salesperson through a genuine renewing of your mind. If I'm not mistaken, I believe your next appointment is with Lew; I wish you all the best with that. Now, let's get out to the first tee!

"Well done!"

Endings... and Beginnings

*You can't go back and change the past, but you can start
where you are.*

— C. S. Lewis

Back with Lew

ALMOST THREE WEEKS after his last meeting with John Philips, Paul was once again headed to meet with Lew. As he walked across Petra's campus at a leisurely pace on a spectacularly bright and sunny Friday morning towards the end of June, it dawned on him how totally different his life was than the last meeting he had had with Lew. Paul smiled to himself as he reflected upon how much things had changed. His relationships with his customers, his coworkers, and most of all his family were now steeped in the deep, meaningful mindset of serving others.

He paused for a moment for no other purpose than to take in the beauty of the morning. He took a deep breath of the fresh spring morning with the wonderful aroma of flowers in bloom and the new beginnings the change of seasons promises. Paul couldn't help but think of how he was a totally different from that self-absorbed, arrogant, and abrasive person that had hurried through the rain that cold and dreary day last October. It occurred to him that this beautiful day was not only indicative of his mood but of his brand-new outlook on life and his role of being a Serving Salesperson.

Lew had asked to meet Paul for lunch, so he entered the building, got on the elevator, and rode up to Lew's floor.

"Good morning, Beth, and how's the best administrative assistant in the entire world this morning?" Paul said with a grin as he approached Lew's assistant.

"I don't know. When I find her, I'll ask her," Beth shot back with her ever-present smile, which seemed brighter and more radiant than ever. "Lew's expecting you. He said to send you right in."

Paul walked confidently into Lew's office where Lew was waiting to greet him.

"Paul! It's so wonderful to see you! I can't tell you how much I've been looking forward to this meeting," Lew said, clasping both of his hands around Paul's outstretched hand. "I've heard nothing but glowing reports from all the members of the TBS about their meetings with you. They were all very impressed with your desire to learn about becoming a Serving Salesperson and with the dedication and intensity with which you undertook all the tasks and exercises they gave you. Sit down and let's go through your notebook and tell me what you've learned."

They both got totally lost in Paul's story of his journey on the road to becoming a Serving Salesperson. Paul burst forth with excitement and enthusiasm as he recounted the key points from his meetings with members of the TBS from Matthew to John and how all of it had deeply impacted virtually every aspect of his life. Paul's excitement grew as he reviewed each completed exercise and paused to tell how each exercise had changed the way he thought about his customers, his coworkers, his family, and anyone else that he felt might be affected.

Lew listened intently, his smile growing ever broader with each story and anecdote Paul told. As Paul finished recounting his meetings with John Philips about guiding the transformation, Lew spoke up.

"Well, Paul, did you finish the last exercise?"

"You know, Lew, once I got to thinking about it, it came to me pretty easily. Here let me show you."

Paul took a sheet of paper from the back of his notebook and handed Lew his idea of how the Seven Pillars of being a Serving Salesperson fit together. Lew didn't think his smile could get any broader, but when he saw what was on the sheet of paper Paul handed him, it did.

On the sheet of paper was a diagram of the Seven Pillars in a circle with another circle with the title "The Serving Salesperson" over the top of the Pillars.

The Seven Pillars of a Serving Salesperson

Lew studied the graphics for a minute. Then looking up he said, "Tell me what your thinking is behind this diagram."

"A thought that kept coming back to me during all of my interviews," said Paul, "was how all the Pillars were intertwined and kept building on each other. While each Pillar has its own distinct principles, they are all connected and provide a framework to support the overlaying philosophy of being a Serving Salesperson.

"A circle is continuous with no beginning and no end," said Paul, "and that's how I now view my role as a Serving Salesperson—continuous, with no end. To be a true Serving Salesperson means to serve each customer to the best of your ability. The work of first transforming your relationship with the customer and then guiding them into transforming themselves has no end, so it's a circle. While there are distinct Pillars, they all support the overlaying philosophy and our primary role of being a Serving Salesperson."

After a while Lew looked up, still beaming. It was a while before he spoke.

"I knew you could do it, Paul," he said softly. "I knew if you took the time, learned from experienced and committed individuals, and studied about how to be a Serving Salesperson, that you could do it."

"I think anyone can," answered Paul, "but the renewing of your mind is a long-term, never-ending process. I don't know if it will take everyone as long as it did me, but I'm sure grateful that I had the benefit of all that time to interview those members of the TBS, to do those exercises, and to get continued coaching from them. By the way, when are you going to tell me what TBS means?"

"All in good time, my friend, all in good time. And there's one other thing."

"What's that?"

"Jim Walters called this morning, and Walters Enterprises is very pleased with the process you set up for the lubricants for their laser cutters," Lew smiled again. "Jim said the production people would like you to come back and look at a couple of other issues they're having. He also told me, 'Maybe there's something to this Serving Salesperson thing after all. Can you talk to me about it?' And guess who I'm going to send over to do that?"

Now it was Paul's turn to smile.

"Boy, the time has really flown by this morning," said Lew, looking at his watch. "Shall we go to lunch?"

"The pleasure would be all mine," said Paul. "Where would you like to go?"

"I hope you don't mind," said Lew with a sudden twinkle in his eye, "but I've invited a few friends to have lunch with us."

A Surprise

Rather than walking to the elevator Lew led Paul down the hall toward the executive conference room. Opening the doors, all the members of the TBS that Paul had interviewed were there to greet him. Lydia, Martha, Phoebe, Matthew, Marcos, Luke, and John were all there waiting for him with big smiles on their faces. Paul spent the next few minutes going around the room, greeting and thanking each one. He felt like it was a homecoming.

After giving Paul ample time to greet and chat briefly with each person, Lew gathered everyone together and simply said, "Shall we eat?"

Lew offered a blessing, thanking God for the food and for helping Paul on the journey along his own road to becoming a Serving Salesperson. Rather than simply ignoring Lew's prayer as he would have done in the past, Paul found himself flooded with gratitude. Suddenly it hit him that his mind had truly been renewed. He had become a Serving Salesperson who was focused not only on serving his customers but on transforming his relationship with them, and then guiding them to elevate their thinking from problems to possibilities and undertaking their own transformation. He also realized that the professional, personal, and even the spiritual transformation he was now feeling was due almost entirely to the people around the table. Just as his mind had been transformed, he felt his heart had also been transformed into a heart of being a Serving Salesperson. His sense of gratitude grew even more.

As the dessert plates were being cleared away. Lew spoke up.

"Well, Paul, now it's time."

"Time for what?" Paul answered. He had been so surprised by meeting again with the members of the TBS that he wasn't sure he could take any more surprises.

"Time to learn what TBS means."

"Finally! I can't tell you how often, especially in the past few weeks, I've thought about this!"

"Matthew, would you do the honors?" asked Lew.

"I'd be delighted to," answered Matthew, standing to address the group. "Paul, TBS stands for the Towel and Basin Society. Do you remember what Jesus did for his closest friends when they shared their last supper together?"

"Hmm," Paul said, thinking for a moment. "Well, when I was a kid, I remember seeing a play at vacation Bible school where Jesus poured water into a basin, washed everybody's feet on stage, and then dried their feet with a towel. I never really got it. The whole thing seemed kind of strange to me."

"Gotta agree with you there," Matthew chuckled. "It does seem odd. Maybe a bit of context might help. Do you know why that simple act has had so much significance that we've named our society after it?"

Paul thought for a minute. "Because it's an act of servanthood?"

"It was that and much more," Mathew continued. "It was truly the ultimate act of being a servant. In Jesus' time, if someone was invited to dinner, the custom was to bathe beforehand. However, after walking through the dusty streets, their feet would be very dirty. So, after they entered their host's house, a servant would be there with a towel and basin to wash their feet. This act was performed by the servant with the lowest standing in the home. It was the job no one wanted. But Jesus willingly volunteered to do that task during the last meal He and His friends shared together. He did it to demonstrate His fond affection for you and me, and the deep value He holds for each one of us. Everything Jesus did reflected other-centered sacrificial love. As it says in Mark

10:45, 'He came not to be served but to serve', and that's the model of the TBS."

Matthew continued. "Just as everything Jesus did was based around serving others, the Serving Salesperson adopts that same mindset toward serving our customers. Unfortunately, a lot of salespeople do not think that way. We think of ourselves as having a towel wrapped around our waist and carrying a basin of water ready to serve our customers. We focus on putting their needs above ours, of coming to them with the attitude of not serving our own needs but serving their needs."

Paul sat silently, reflecting on Matthew's words. After pausing for a moment, he spoke up. "Now it all makes sense to me," he said softly. "I can see how using the model of serving that Jesus lived should be the foundation of serving others' needs rather than your own."

Lew stood up to speak.

"And now, Paul, we have a little something for you," he said walking over to where Paul was sitting. "You've earned it, and more than that, you've lived it." He reached down and pinned something on the lapel of Paul's jacket. Looking down, Paul saw a gold lapel pin with the three letters *TBS* engraved on it. "You're now an official member of the TBS, Paul. Welcome! Well done, good and faithful servant!" The entire group gave him applause.

As the lunch was breaking up, Marcos Simón lingered a bit.

"Paul, I have this salesperson who is, well, with him it's 'all about me.' I was wondering, would you talk to him about what you've learned?"

"I would consider it an honor," answered Paul. "How does next Tuesday morning at 9:00 sound?"

"He'll be here," answered Marcos with a smile.

Reflections

Back in Lew's office, Paul realized how emotionally spent he had become.

"Lew, I really don't know what to say. The last time we met, you could have fired me and would have been totally justified in doing so.

And if you would have done that, I'd have found another sales job and would have continued in my self-centered, arrogant, and abrasive, ways. I just can't thank you enough for believing in me, for putting your faith in me."

"Paul, it's truly been my privilege. I simply provided you with tools. You're the one who chose to keep the faith and consistently use those tools day after day. Always remember that mustard seed faith can move mountains," Lew continued, encouraging Paul.

Paul soaked up Lew's every word, gratefully nodding in agreement.

"I understand that you're seeing much more of your wife these days," said Lew, with a twinkle in his eye.

"That's right, Lew. Learning to be a Serving Salesperson has had a wonderful impact on my family. We see each other more, we talk more, we spend time together with our children. It's like falling in love all over again. And with this Sunday being Father's Day, she's invited me over to her—I mean our—house for brunch after church."

"I hope everything goes well," said Lew. "I have a feeling it will."

"I have something to do first, though," said Paul. "I am going to see our minister to talk about a decision I want to make."

Father's Day

That Sunday was Father's Day, and it was a bright and beautiful summer morning as Paul picked up Mary and the girls for church. The girls were both arrayed in beautiful summer dresses and Paul marveled at how both were growing into young ladies. Mary looked absolutely radiant in a beautiful red dress that Paul could tell was new.

As they sat in church, Paul felt a wonderful sense of peace come over him, something that he hadn't felt in a long time. The sermon was entitled "Becoming the Father You Truly Can Be," and the minister finished his sermon by reading passages from Ephesians 5:25, 28: "Husbands, love your wives just as Christ loved the church ... In this same way, husbands ought to love their wives as their own bodies. He who loves his wife loves himself."

With that, Paul reached over and took Mary's hand, which she gladly accepted and proceeded to hold in both of hers for the rest of the service.

Arriving back at the house, Mary insisted on Paul sitting in the recliner with a cup of coffee while she and the girls prepared brunch. As he sat reading his phone with Gracie snuggled happily in his lap and Alex curled up at his feet, Paul could hear the girls giggling with excitement and a couple of times he heard Ruthie whisper, "Now, Mom?" He pretended not to hear as Mary shushed her each time.

"Brunch is ready in the dining room," Mary called.

The dining room? We almost never eat in the dining room! We only eat in there when it's something really special! Paul thought.

As Paul walked into the dining room, he was taken aback by what he saw. The table was set beautifully with their wedding china, silver, and crystal. There was a gorgeous floral centerpiece, and looking at the serving dishes on the table Paul could see all his favorites, things Mary hadn't prepared for him in a long time.

Mary offered a beautiful blessing over the food, and the girls took turns serving their father. As Paul looked across the table at Mary then at the girls and feeling the dogs underfoot, he found himself thinking, *This seems right. This is way things should be.* However, he wasn't sure what to do or say. Things were going well, but still he wasn't sure what he should do next, how to make happen what he wanted to happen.

After the dishes had been cleared away, the time came for cards and gifts. There were funny cards from the girls, and a beautiful one from Mary with a heartfelt sentiment. "To the man I love" it said on the outside. He opened it up and it read: "You are my blessing from God, and I thank Him every day for you." Paul literally didn't know what to say. After a moment he looked up and said, "I love you, Mary," his voice cracking.

There was only one gift, a beautifully wrapped small box. As Paul took off the wrapping paper, he noticed it was a jewelry box. What could it be? A watch? He already had a nice one. Some piece of jewelry? The only other jewelry he had was his wedding ring, and he didn't really wear anything else.

With a mixture of nervousness and anticipation, he opened the box.

Inside was a beautiful brass keychain with a shiny new brass key that he instantly recognized as the key to their house. The keychain had a beautiful round dark blue onyx stone set inside a brass setting with the single word *Daddy* inscribed in gold cursive letters diagonally across the front. Paul looked up in surprise, totally speechless as the girls shouted in unison, "Welcome home, Daddy!" He suddenly and unexpectedly found himself overcome with a wave of emotion and to his surprise felt tears welling up in his eyes. He looked over at Mary and saw her eyes were also glistening, with tears running down her cheeks.

She slowly got up, walked over to him, bent over, and cupped his head in her hands. She then gave him a soft, gentle, lingering kiss. "Yes, Daddy," she said, slowly lifting her face away from his, still cupping his head and wiping the tears off his cheeks with her thumbs.

"Welcome home."

Acknowledgments

First off, I want to thank my wife, Cathy, whose love, support, patience, inspiration and encouragement inspired me to keep the faith through the many hours of working in this book.

And I'm so grateful to our children, Megan and Jennifer, and our grandchildren, Cambrie, Olivia, Clarke, and Riley, who all bring joy into our lives.

I couldn't have written this book without the assistance from my long-term colleagues at the Lacy School of Business at Butler University, Robert Mackoy, Ph.D., Professor Emeritus of Marketing from the Lacy School of Business at Butler, and Lova Randrianasolo, Ph.D. Professor of Marketing at the Quinlan School of Business, Loyola University of Chicago. Bob and Lova worked tireless hours with me designing and administering the questionnaire that surveyed B2B buyers. They then worked equally as tirelessly analyzing the data that was used to formulate the Seven Pillars of a Serving Salesperson. This book would not have been possible without their amazing talents and efforts.

I'm grateful for the many former students from my time at Indiana University, Butler University, Purdue University, and the University of Notre Dame as well as the large number of business acquaintances that I interviewed to provide the information for the questionnaire used in our research.

I appreciate the team at Illumify Media—Michael Klassen, Jen Clark, Valerie Morris, and Geoff Stone—who truly did bring this book to life. I couldn't have done it without you, folks!

I'd also like to thank two very talented graphic artists, Rhiain Coslett and Travis Collins, who provided the illustrations used in this book. And finally, I wish to acknowledge the contributions of my late brother, James, a talented architect and graphic artist who provided the ideas for the illustrations as well as advice and counsel during the early drafts of the book. He was gone too soon. We miss you Jamo.